Total War

New Perspectives on W

MW00490417

Series Editors

MICHAEL A. BARNHART, SUNY at Stony Brook
H. P. WILLMOTT

The Second World War, a conflict that literally spanned the globe, has spawned the publication of thousands of books. In fact, it seems that new ones appear almost daily. Why, then, another series on this subject? Because there is a need for brief, accessible, and affordable books that synthesize the best of recent scholarship on World War II. This series aims to differ from the vast majority of volumes published on the war. Marked by tightly focused studies on vital aspects of the conflict, from the war against Japan to the Anglo-American alliance to the rise of the Red Army, the books in this provocative new series will compel World War II scholars, students, and buffs to consider old questions in new terms. Covering significant topics—battles and campaigns, world leaders, and political and social dimensions—*Total War* intends to be lively, engaging, and instructive.

Volumes Published

H. P. Willmott, *The War with Japan: The Period of Balance, May 1942–October 1943* (2002). Cloth ISBN 0-8420-5032-9   Paper ISBN 0-8420-5033-7

THE WAR WITH JAPAN

THE WAR WITH JAPAN

THE PERIOD OF BALANCE
MAY 1942–OCTOBER 1943

H. P. WILLMOTT

Total War
New Perspectives on World War II
NO. 1

A Scholarly Resources Inc. Imprint
Wilmington, Delaware

Scholarly Resources Inc.
104 Greenhill Avenue
Wilmington, DE 19805-1897
www.scholarly.com

Library of Congress Cataloging-in-Publication Data

Willmott, H. P.
  The war with Japan : the period of balance, May 1942–October 1943 /
H. P. Willmott.
    p. cm. — (Total war ; no. 1)
  Includes bibliographical references and index.
  ISBN 0-8420-5032-9 — ISBN 0-8420-5033-7 (pbk. : alk. paper)
  1. World War, 1939–1945—Campaigns—Pacific Area. 2. World War,
1939–1945—Japan. I. Title. II. Series.

D767 .W48 2002
940.54'26—dc21   2002017617

About the Author

H. P. Willmott is a senior research fellow at the Institute for the Study of War and Society, De Montfort University, and a visiting lecturer at Greenwich Maritime Institute, University of Greenwich. He holds master's degrees from Liverpool and National Defense and a doctorate from London Universities. A fellow of the Royal Historical Society, he has served on the faculties of Temple University, the University of Memphis, and the Department of Military Strategy and Operations, National War College. He has written extensively on modern naval and military subjects including *Empires in the Balance, The Barrier and the Javelin, Grave of a Dozen Schemes, The Second World War in the Far East*, and the critically acclaimed *The Great Crusade: A New Complete History of the Second World War*. His *Pearl Harbor*, published in 2001, challenged many of the assumptions made about this operation. Formerly with reserve airborne forces, he is the author of the forthcoming *When Men Lost Faith in Reason: Reflections on Warfare in the Twentieth Century*. Married with one wife, two children, two dogs, one mortgage, and an accountant to support, Willmott has one medal and no prospects.

Contents

Maps

Introduction

Europeans date World War II from 1939 to 1945 and, with North Americans, date the Japanese part of that conflict from December 1941 to August 1945. The Japanese official histories date it from September 1931 and the start of the campaign in Manchuria; and, if such a date for the outbreak of the war would not command much sympathy in Western histories, there might well be more than a passing sympathy with any account that sought to establish July 1937, and the beginning of the China war, as the real start of the Second World War. In fact, with such a date the Japanese war is endowed with terms of reference that make sense because, in reality, after December 1941 Japan found itself involved, in geographical terms, in three quite separate wars: in eastern Asia, specifically within China; in Southeast Asia; and in the Pacific. The opening of Japan's war with the United States, Britain, and the Netherlands in effect marked the point of transition from what was largely a continental war, fought with characteristics of mass, to one that primarily embraced naval and maritime dimensions. After December 1941 the Asian war and the naval and maritime conflicts in the western Pacific and Southeast Asia were largely separated from one another, at least in terms of their common outcome being unrelated and not immediately interdependent.

This widening of the war in which Japan found itself in December 1941 resulted in a series of victories throughout Southeast Asia that were, both individually and collectively, impressive. In the three weeks following the attack on Pearl Harbor by aircraft from the First Carrier Striking Force, Japanese land, sea, and air forces won a series of engagements that effectively decided these campaigns, if indeed their outcome had not been decided beforehand in the sense that Japan's enemies were defeated before the first shots were fired. With scarcely any margin of superiority over the various military forces in Southeast Asia, the Japanese established the basis of victory by virtue of possession of the initiative and on account of naval and air superiority, advantages of concentration, and local superiority against enemies defensively dispersed. To this, one could add the critical advantage of surprise, were it not for the fact that the Japanese did not so much surprise as amaze enemies that simply could not comprehend either the quality of Japan's armed forces or a string of offensive operations that unfolded across 122 degrees of longitude. These operations possessed a coherence and an economy of effort that were striking and not in any way demeaned by the evident unpreparedness of Japan's enemies and their inability to coordinate their individual, failing efforts.

This period of Japanese success in Southeast Asia and the western Pacific had more or less run its course by May 1942. Thereafter the Japanese registered the occasional offensive victory but, in real terms, the period of conquest came to an end in May 1942. In this month, and in the one that followed it, were fought two battles that arose from decisions made by both the Japanese and American high commands that postdated the outbreak of war in December 1941. The battles, fought in the Coral Sea in May and off Midway Islands in June 1942, represented the first engagements that were not the result of decisions taken by Tokyo before the start of war; and their result, collectively, was to impose a halt upon proceedings as both sides were obliged to consider their next moves in a situation wholly different from what had prevailed prior to these actions. The most important, immediate, and obvious result of these two battles was, to borrow an analogy, that the strategic initiative was like a gun lying in the street: it was there for either side to pick up and use. In the aftermath of the battle off Midway, and at a time when negotiations with Britain brought the American high command to the realization that there could be no move against German-controlled northwest Europe in 1942, the Americans came to the decision to move against Japanese positions in the lower Solomons.

Thus was earmarked one of the two battlefields of this second phase of the Pacific war, the other being eastern New Guinea where the Japanese, in the aftermath of the defeat at Midway, undertook an offensive that aimed to eliminate the possibility of an Allied threat materializing from this area. The two campaigns developed more or less in tandem, and in this fact was part of the explanation of the

Japanese defeat in both theaters in the seven or eight months after Midway. What is most curious about the Japanese defeat in the Solomons is that their strategic policy for a war with the United States was predicated upon the securing of certain island groups and bases on which the Imperial armed forces were to found their defense of the home islands and acquired "southern resources area." The Japanese planned to use land-based aircraft from neighboring bases and island groups, plus the fleet, to support formations and bases brought under attack and to fight the Americans to exhaustion, the point being that the various parts of the defense—the forward base, the supporting elements, and the fleet component—would be mutually supportive and would together provide overall numerical superiority relative to an enemy amphibious assault certain to possess initial numerical superiority over any single part of the Japanese defense. The lower Solomons campaign, August 1942 to February 1943, was the only occasion during the Pacific war when the basic Japanese concept of a campaign was vindicated—but by the Americans who, by seizing the airfield on Guadalcanal, imposed upon the Japanese the battle that the latter had expected to fail.

These two campaigns, in the lower Solomons and along the Kakoda Trail for control of eastern New Guinea, combined with the battles in the Coral Sea and off Midway Islands, form the watershed of the Pacific war. In the first of these, the campaign for control of Guadalcanal, there were more than fifty actions involving aircraft or warships of two prewar navies, and together these battles and campaigns saw the Imperial Navy (Kaigun) and U.S. Navy fight one another, and themselves, to exhaustion. The two navies fought a series of battles in which fortune changed sides but in which victories and defeats were mingled with losses that ultimately were prohibitive, and herein was the significance of the period between February and October 1943. In these nine months very few islands changed hands. The U.S. forces eliminated Japanese holdings in the Aleutians and in the central Solomons, and in eastern New Guinea the Americans and their allies began the move beyond Huon Gulf and into the Markham valley. But in these months the U.S. Navy took delivery of the first of the warships that were to carry the fight to the Japanese home islands, and in that fact was the point of the next phase of the war, after November 1943. In this next phase a fleet that was increasingly a wartime creation—a fleet built in the period of hostilities—with ever-growing ease outfought an enemy navy that could not match its opponent in terms of numbers and quality for two obvious reasons. First, the five carrier task groups that opened the Iwo Jima campaign in February 1945 with an attack on Honshu numbered 119 warships, of which just two carriers, two battleships, and two heavy cruisers entered service before Pearl Harbor, and this at a time when the Kaigun had all but ceased to exist. Second, the attack on the Gilbert and Ellice Islands in November 1943 marked the stage where the outcome of the war, in terms of the certainty of decision, was reached because the Americans, in contrast to the events of August 1942 in the lower Solomons, attacked with such superiority of numbers as to ensure the overwhelming of individual bases and their simultaneous isolation from outside support. What remained thereafter, as the Americans moved in strength that was unchallengeable, were questions of the timing and exact nature of Japan's defeat and the cost that would be exacted in the process.

There was another dimension to this conflict, however, the campaign against Japanese shipping. At the time when Japan went to war in December 1941 it needed some 10 million tons of shipping to meet its requirements but had a little over 6 million tons under its own flag. Here was a recipe for disaster even without the Imperial Navy's calculation, made in mid-1941, that assessed the replacement capacity of Japanese shipyards at 900,000 tons per year, or 75,000 tons per month, which oddly was the amount of shipping that the Kaigun estimated could be expected to be lost to an American submarine campaign. Leaving aside such a strange coincidence, both the losses incurred by the Japanese by October 1943 and the current rate of losses by this time had reached critical proportions. Such facts were the reasons for the Imperial Navy's introduction of general convoy during and after November 1943, but during 1944 the Japanese position in effect collapsed. Despite output being more than double what had been estimated to be the maximum capability of Japanese yards, shipping losses also doubled, to more than four times the figure that had been designated as worst-case losses, while the figures for output were misleading: the unprecedented level of building was only possible by denial to existing shipping of overhauls, refits, and repairs.

Japanese Shipping Losses by Comparative Periods between 7 December 1941 and 31 October 1943 (by number of ships and tonnage)

	7 Dec. 1941– 30 Apr. 1942	1 May 1942– 28 Feb. 1943	1 Mar. 1943– 31 Oct. 1943
Naval shipping	21: 96,726	61: 310,801	67: 382,561
Military shipping	21: 108,868	64: 322,407	93: 296,836
Civilian shipping	16: 70,488	89: 345,982	111: 379,199
Total losses	58: 276,082	214: 979,190	271: 1,058,596
Average monthly losses	12.1: 57,830	21.4: 97,919	33.9: 132,325

Clearly, the Japanese had some way to go along this particular road to defeat by the end of this second period of this war, but the critical point about this period is that at sea Japan's defeat had both naval and maritime dimensions, and both became discernible at this time. Japan, uniquely, could have been beaten by a naval effort that left its merchant shipping intact, and it could have been beaten by a *guerre de course* against its shipping that left its main fleet strength unreduced: it was subjected to a total defeat that at sea embraced both its naval and merchant fleets. Elsewhere it was a defeat that manifested itself in Burma, southern China, and Manchuria with Japanese defeats in the field. Moreover, it found Japan in effect without allies and left the nation without any genuine popular support throughout the conquered territories of eastern and Southeast Asia. *The War with Japan: The Period of Balance, May 1942–October 1943* concerns itself with virtually all of these aspects of Japan's defeat, with those on the mainland excluded, because in this period of balance its various elements assumed shape and substance. Certain aspects of defeat were military; others took the form of conferences that set out the course of defeat for Japan and, for that matter, of Germany and Italy. All aspects of defeat and victory were present in this second phase of the Pacific war, but it is the decisions of the victor of the moment, in January 1942, that the reader is now invited to consider.

I

The

Gun

in

the

Street

1

APPRECIATING THE SITUATION

In the three weeks following the Pearl Harbor attack, Japanese forces won a series of victories throughout Southeast Asia that effectively decided these several campaigns. With hardly any margin of superiority over the various enemy forces in this theater, the Japanese established the basis of victory on account of advantages of concentration, possession of the initiative, and local superiority against enemies defensively dispersed. American acknowledgment of defeat in this opening phase was provided in this time. The decision to divert a seven-ship military convoy bound for the Philippines to Suva, and then to Brisbane, was tacit recognition that the Philippines would be lost and that defeat in Southeast Asia was unavoidable. The American forces, once they arrived in Australia, were sent northward to Port Moresby in eastern New Guinea and to Darwin, and there were various proposals of establishing a route to the Philippines from the south. But the logic of the situation was remorseless and irresistible; and as reality asserted itself, attention shifted to the question of operations once the initial phase of the war was complete.

In no small measure the United States held the power of decision for the various allied nations opposed to Japan. It was not one nation, however, but twenty-six that on 1 January 1942, with the Japanese poised to move into the oil-rich Dutch East Indies, declared themselves to be the United Nations committed not to make a separate peace with any of their enemies. By their declaration the United Nations served notice on Tokyo of fundamental error even in its moment of triumph; the terms of reference of a Pacific war were not Japan's to determine.

NO OBSERVATION BETTER DEFINES what is usually the root cause of failure in war than Carl von Clausewitz's: "the first, the grandest, and most decisive act of judgment which the Statesman and General exercises is rightly to understand [the nature of] the War in which he engages, not to take it for something, or wish to make of it something, which it is not . . . and it is impossible for it to be." Japan went to war in December 1941 with the hope that it could fight the United States to a standstill that would leave it with its conquests in Southeast Asia intact. Leaving aside the fact that hope is a poor basis of a war plan, the Japanese with the power of decision assumed, inasfar as the eventuality was considered at all, that the war thus initiated would have limited terms of reference set by Tokyo. But no single nation ever wholly determines the terms of reference of a war, and while the Japanese could never properly recognize the possibility of defeat—a nation that had no experience of defeat could not envisage failure—the basic point was that for their high command the alternative to victory in a limited war necessarily had to be Japan's defeat in a limited war. In reality, the alternative to victory in a limited war was defeat in a total war, and it was the latter, or at least its prospect, that presented itself in the United Nations declaration. It was a prospect that at this time seemed to offer the certainty of the destruction not simply of the Imperial armed services but also of the Imperial system itself.

Thus the Japanese high command was obliged to turn its attention to the question of operations in the next phase of the war even as its victory in Southeast Asia assumed reality. In effect, the high command was most concerned about the Imperial Navy, and naturally so: its raison d'être was wholly concerned with fighting a defensive war in the Pacific. Underpinning all Kaigun calculations was the awareness that it could not match the U.S. Navy in numbers, but numbers were the essence in Kaigun planning for an American war. Its basic idea was to impose an attritional battle on an enemy force moving across the western Pacific by subjecting it to attack by submarines and land-based aircraft. With the enemy thus weakened, battle would be joined with light forces backed by cruisers and fast battleships, making two or perhaps three massed torpedo attacks at night on the enemy battle line. In addition, the Kaigun planned to use aircraft carriers to neutralize U.S. carriers and thereby deprive the American battle force of deep reconnaissance capability before the main battle was joined. With all of its battleships rebuilt in the course of the 1930s in the search for extra speed, with additional armor, and with enhanced range as gun elevations were increased, the Kaigun anticipated its battle divisions fighting a disorganized and depleted enemy at a range beyond effective American response, this being an action that would result in decisive American defeat.

Such was the Kaigun's basic battle plan for much of the interwar period, and continuity can be seen in terms of the subsequent plan of campaign of the years immediately before the outbreak of the Pacific war. With the entry into service of long-range shore-based aircraft and new classes of command, scouting, and attack submarines, the area of battle moved eastward, from the general area of the Bonins. With the decision to fortify the Marshalls, previously prohibited since the islands were mandated from the League of Nations, the Kaigun planned for battle across a greater depth than hitherto possible. But both separately and together, these plans invite comment on two levels.

First, whatever relevance the battle plan possessed in the 1920s was largely past by the latter part of the 1930s. The idea of massed torpedo attacks at night certainly was relevant, as the U.S. Navy found to its cost in the Solomons campaign in 1942, but the new tactical formations that began to appear in the 1930s really marked the point where the Kaigun's concept of the future battle faltered: widely separated task groups, with few major units, presented a very different problem than the massed battle lines of history.

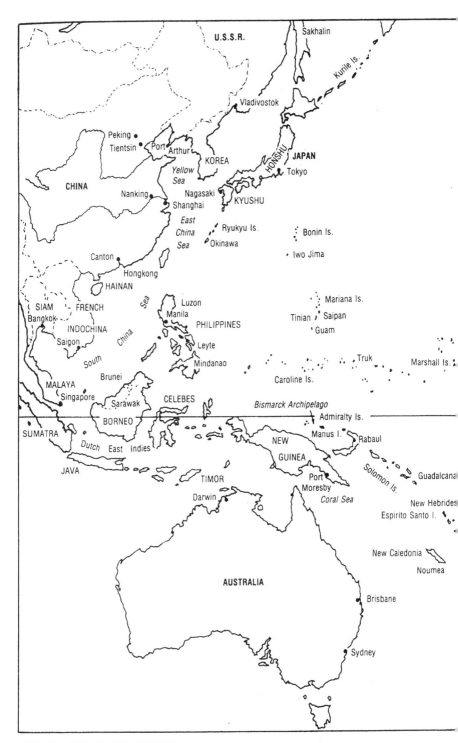

GENERAL MAP OF THE PACIFIC

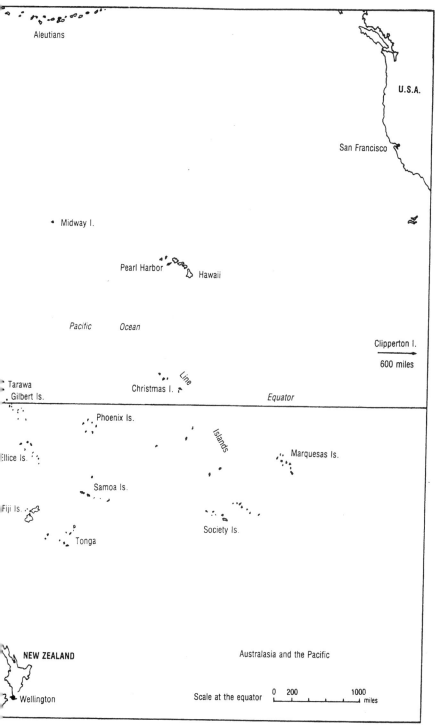

Aleutians

U.S.A.

San Francisco

Midway I.

Pearl Harbor Hawaii

Pacific Ocean

Clipperton I.
600 miles

Tarawa
Gilbert Is.
Christmas I.
Line
Equator

Phoenix Is.

Islands

Ellice Is.
Marquesas Is.

Samoa Is.

Fiji Is.
Society Is.

Tonga

NEW ZEALAND
Australasia and the Pacific

Wellington
Scale at the equator   0   200   1000
                                            miles

From H. P. Willmott, *The Barrier and the Javelin: Japanese and Allied Pacific Strategies, February to June 1942* (Annapolis: Naval Institute Press, 1983), xviii–xix.

Second, and more serious, what was in reality a tactical plan for the conduct of battle by some mysterious process akin to transubstantiation became the basis of national security strategy. Herein was evidence that the Kaigun never understood the difference between war and a war, between a war and a campaign, between a campaign and a battle: by some process that defies understanding, the Imperial Navy identified them as one and the same. Moreover, the individual parts of this plan do not bear close scrutiny while, incredibly, the basic plan itself was never subjected to fleet exercise. Various individual parts of the plan were subjected to exercise and, most interestingly, the submarine dimension was proved wanting. In 1939 it was found that Japanese submarines would not be able to mount successive attacks on American task groups as had been assumed. The result was that the terms of reference were amended in 1940 exercises in order to ensure that they could, but when they failed again the *Kaigun* went to war on the assumption that "it would be all right on the night": it was thought that submarines would be able to inflict half of all enemy losses before battle was joined. But by 1941 the plan had been developed to include the securing of a perimeter defense on which the Kaigun would fight the Americans to exhaustion, yet in the vastness of the distances that separated the Aleutians and Solomons and New Britain and the Andamans any perimeter necessarily consisted mostly of gaps. These gaps were occasionally separated by individual bases that lacked the strength sufficient to allow the Kaigun to oppose an enemy with the choice of when, in what strength, and where to undertake the offensive. Moreover, the Kaigun, which in the late 1930s did not have the means to fortify its existing holdings properly, could hardly prepare new bases across thousands of extra miles of ocean; and, perhaps even more serious, it could not guarantee to be able to hold intact battle and carrier formations ready to meet enemy moves. By adopting a defensive policy, the Kaigun condemned itself to dispersal, which was certain to erode its strength at the point of contact.

How well this situation was understood within the Japanese high command is unknown. Certain individuals such as Vice Admiral Inoue Shigeyoshi, who was to command naval forces in the southwest Pacific, most definitely did read it correctly, but he was generally regarded as unsound—partly because he was "air-minded" but also because of his often-expressed conviction that war with the United States had to be avoided. Among the naval high command as 1941 gave way to 1942

there was a general awareness that Japan, contrary to its original intention, could not assume the defensive at the end of first-phase operations: retention of the initiative and offensive operations represented
the only means whereby the enemy's declared intention not to accept
a negotiated settlement could be broken. The Japanese problem, however, was which offensive option should be adopted: the naval high
command was institutionally divided between the Naval Ministry and
Naval General Staff on the one side and the Combined Fleet staff on
the other, and there was no overall sense of urgency in the first weeks
of 1942. It was not until April, in the aftermath of the Doolittle Raid,
that a sense of urgency communicated itself throughout the Kaigun,
although by that time the decisions that led to the battles of the Coral
Sea and Midway had been taken.

IN THE WEEKS OF DISCUSSION that preceded these decisions, the
attack on Pearl Harbor, with which Japan initiated hostilities against
the United States, was critically important. Sufficient attention has
been paid by History to this event to allow these pages to record just
one fact: the attack was a failure. Eighteen American ships were either
sunk or damaged, but the carriers, by virtue of their absence, escaped
without loss, as did the submarines; left untouched were the power
station, docks, and oil depot of the naval base. In the immediate aftermath of the attack Japanese naval attention centered on the fact that
no American carrier had been sunk, and from this fact emerged the calculation that the Kaigun had to complete the task left unfinished at
Pearl Harbor: the American carriers had to be brought to battle and destroyed. This calculation, however, was accompanied by another,
much wider one, which held that the real error of 7 December was not
that there had been no second, followup strike: no provision had
been made for an invasion of Oahu and occupation of the naval base.
The simple fact was that the demands of the various campaigns in
Southeast Asia made it impossible for the Japanese to undertake
an amphibious assault in the central Pacific at the same time as the
effort in the intended "southern resources area" unfolded: the divisions
and shipping needed for such an assault had been beyond Japan's
means.

Thus, from virtually the outset of the war, the need for offensive action and the Hawaiian option were under consideration within the Kaigun, but by the beginning of 1942 four offensive options presented themselves. The first concerned Australia. Prewar Kaigun thinking had envisaged American use of Australia as the base for a "roll-back" strategy, hence the decision to secure Rabaul as an outpost to Truk and the Indies. Indications that the Americans did indeed view Australia in such terms led the naval staff to favor this option. The obvious problems were the question of whether northern or the whole of Australia should be the object of Japanese ambitions, plus the distances involved in any such undertaking.

The second option envisaged a Japanese effort in the southwest Pacific with the aim of cutting American lines of communication between Pearl Harbor and eastern Australia. This option emerged as an alternative to the second, one that would be argued if the second option was discounted. The third option was for an offensive into the Indian Ocean with the possibility of a linkup with Germany and Italy, with which Japan had concluded the Tripartite Pact on 19 January 1942. This alliance was itself one of the factors that provided the rationale for this option: the collapse of the British position in Malaya, and the anticipation of the early fall of Singapore, offered an extra reason and the opportunity for such an offensive. The fourth and final option emerged after 14 January 1942 when Admiral Yamamoto Isoroku, commander in chief of the Combined Fleet, ordered his staff to examine a central Pacific option. With little possibility of the Imperial Army, the Rikugun, being persuaded to release the divisions needed for an assault on Oahu, this central Pacific option identified Midway and Johnston Islands as Japanese objectives, their being secured as outposts from which an assault on Oahu could be staged.

These options presented the Kaigun with an obvious difficulty: they could not be pursued concurrently or in combination, and there was little possibility of their being mounted consecutively. Each course of action offered the prospect of very real strategic success but not without risk.

The categorical refusal of the Rikugun to consider seriously the Australian and Indian Ocean options meant that both were quickly struck from the strategic agenda. The Australian option was the first to be discounted, killed by the Army's refusal to even consider making available the twelve divisions needed for such an operation. It had only been with great reluctance that the Rikugun had made forces available for the southwest Pacific, and its refusal to commit troops to a major offensive beyond the Malay Barrier was based on the impossibility of being able to sustain a large expeditionary force at so great a distance from the home islands. This logic was unanswerable and by the end of January 1942 the Australia option was dead, although it was not until 7 March that the Army formally vetoed this proposal.

The Indian Ocean option proved to have a more tenacious grip on life. Planning was sufficiently advanced by the first week of February for representatives of both services' staffs to be invited to Yamamoto's flagship for three days of discussions and war games that began on 20 February, two days after the German naval attaché in Tokyo reported to Berlin that the Japanese had made inquiries about a joint German-Japanese move to secure Madagascar. In fact, on the previous day, the 17th, the Germans had made available to the Japanese all information in their possession on the subject of landing sites on Ceylon.

The seeming attractiveness of the Indian Ocean option at this time was largely the result of the coming together of four factors. These were the British collapse that resulted in the capitulation at Singapore on 15 February and the fact that a considerable part of Japanese naval strength was in the south and hence could be deployed to the Indian Ocean without undue difficulty. In addition, the obvious attraction of an offensive operation in the Indian Ocean that would round off Japanese victories in Southeast Asia, and the prospects of cooperation between the signatories of the Tripartite Pact, beckoned. In the course of Japanese staff discussions one more consideration emerged. With the Combined Fleet planners thinking in terms of using two divisions to secure Ceylon and to take an outpost in the Chagos Archipelago, the possibility of shattering British prestige and authority in India and throughout the Indian Ocean seemed a likely outcome of a Japanese offensive.

Exactly why this option was discounted is not clear, but suffice to say that by the first week of March the Indian Ocean option, like the Australian option, had been removed from serious consideration, albeit with one caveat: as early as December 1941 the Kaigun considered a single raid into the Indian Ocean at the end of the Japanese conquest of Southeast Asia. When the idea of a major endeavor in the Indian Ocean died, this earlier idea was revived with a provisional timetable set for the first week of April.

Discounting these options was not much help to the Kaigun. It had gone to war with the intention of waging a three-phase conflict, with the second phase to be implemented after 1 April 1942. By the second week of March it had no plan for this second phase and no clear idea of what it might entail other than that it had to involve offensive action but not be directed against Australia or into the Indian Ocean. At this stage, however, the Rikugun, having ensured that it would not be encumbered with any major offensive commitment, was prepared to support the naval staff's idea of an offensive into the southwest Pacific with the aim of securing New Caledonia, Fiji, and Samoa in order to cut American lines of communication with eastern Australia. At the Army-Navy liaison meeting of 13 March the Rikugun endorsed the southwest Pacific option, but by then this particular option had been dismissed as irrelevant by Yamamoto.

BEGINNING IN FEBRUARY 1942, U.S. carrier formations conducted a series of operations against Japanese bases in the central and southwest Pacific. On 1 February, American carriers attacked targets in the Marshalls and Gilberts to no great effect before moving to cover U.S. troop movements in the south Pacific. On 17 February one carrier formation sailed from the New Hebrides for an attack on Rabaul, but, sighted during the approach to contact, it was obliged to fight off attacks by two torpedo-bombers on the 20th and thereafter to abandon its mission. Four days later a second U.S. carrier formation attacked Wake, and on 6 March the two formations effected a rendezvous, two days before Japanese forces came ashore at Lae and Salamaua and at Queen Carola Inlet at Buna in the upper Solomons. On 10 March aircraft from the *Lexington* and *Yorktown* attacked Japanese shipping still in Huon Gulf, accounting for two transports and two escorts: one light cruiser, two destroyers, two minesweepers, and one transport were damaged extensively.

The U.S. Pacific Fleet war diary recorded on 11 March that it was doubtful if the enemy would be greatly inconvenienced by their losses, but the Americans did far better than they realized. With no forward base, the damaged units were forced to return to Japan for repairs, while the loss of the two transports was critical for a command that had been obliged to use the same transports, troops, and escorts for successive operations. For the Japanese high command the lessons of Huon Gulf were obvious: future operations would have to be deliberate affairs if the losses on the scale of 10 March were to be avoided; that the forces available in the southwest Pacific were wholly inadequate and would have to be strengthened; and that the whole concept of offensive operations in the southwest Pacific would have to be rethought, given the revelation that two American carriers were in theater. Inoue asked for carrier reinforcement in the aftermath of the attack, and in so doing he prompted the obvious question: If Japanese carriers were committed to the southwest Pacific, then the operations that would then be put into effect would necessarily be major—indeed, perhaps the major Japanese effort for 1942.

This prospect presented no real difficulty for the naval staff in Tokyo. The idea of an offensive against New Caledonia, Fiji, and Samoa in June or July after Port Moresby and Tulagi had been secured in late May thus took shape, and it received support from the Combined Fleet. Thus, there appeared to be no real basis of dispute between Naval Ministry and staff, theater command and Combined Fleet. By this time, however, Yamamoto had drawn a very different conclusion from U.S. carrier operations in the southwest Pacific: the importance not of the theater but of the carriers. As early as mid-March, in the aftermath of the U.S. carrier raid on Marcus Island some 700 miles from Tokyo (4 March) but at a time when plans for a raid into the Indian Ocean were being finalized and the naval staff was working on the southwest Pacific option, Yamamoto had come to the view that the only way of forcing the American carriers to fight "the decisive battle" was to move beyond the 180th meridian, against U.S. national territory. With the Japanese aware that any attempt to repeat a raid on Pearl Harbor was out of the question, the attention of Yamamoto and his staff naturally turned to Midway, which had been studied as a Japanese objective both before the outbreak of war and during December 1941. In reality there was no target other than Midway that presented itself as the subject of the Combined Fleet's aspirations, and it was with a scheme for the seizure of Midway in the hope of inducing and winning "the decisive battle" that Commander Watanabe Yasuji, Yamamoto's logistics staff officer, confronted his opposite numbers in the plans division of the Naval General Staff at the critical meetings of 2–5 April.

THE CASE AGAINST THE MIDWAY option consisted of two main lines of argument. The first was to dispute the assumption that an assault on Midway was the course of action most likely to provoke decisive battle and the negotiated peace that assured victory would bring. There was nothing to prevent the Americans from writing off Midway in the knowledge that its recovery was assured at a time of their own choosing. To the Naval General Staff, Midway did not have the strategic and political importance that the Yamamoto thesis suggested. To the staff planners in the southwest Pacific were various islands for which the Americans would have to fight, and for the Japanese to attempt to force the issue in this theater there was advantage in the fact that here the lines of communication problems of both sides would be roughly equal: an offensive in the central Pacific, against an atoll 1,323 miles from Pearl Harbor but 2,591 miles from Tokyo, could only ensure that advantages of time and distance lay with the Americans.

The second argument was to challenge the assumption that, once held, Midway would prove an asset. The staff's view was that, if taken, Midway could neither be sustained over a period nor operate effectively as a base. The distances between Midway and Wake and the Aleutians were simply too great to be covered by the number of flying boats that could be gathered in the six square miles of Midway atoll. Moreover, the two square miles of its two islands provided no means of concentrating sufficient aircraft numbers at Midway to guarantee its security.

These were the main lines of argument adopted by the staff planners in dealing with Watanabe, but two other matters also were raised. The first was that a June schedule meant that no more than seven-tenths of the supply needs of a Midway operation could be met. The second was that even if Midway was secured, the formations gathered off the atoll could not sustain themselves on station for more than six days before having to withdraw—that is, Japanese forces would be forced to retire from the area before the decisive battle could be fought. Singly and together, these points were unanswerable, and they should have indicated the adoption of some alternative operation, but the basic point was somewhat different: Yamamoto and his staff were not interested in ensuring policy that emerged as a result of reasoned argument.

The various staff arguments were simply ignored by Watanabe until, on 5 April, he made the whole question one of authority. Yamamoto repeated his views, specifically the assumption that the seizure of Midway would either force a decisive battle or result in major strategic gain. This assumption represented nothing more than dogmatic assertion unsupported by any reasoned argument, and in effect it sidestepped the whole of the naval staff's case and forced a choice between adhering to its original intention and agreement with the Rikugun, at the cost of losing the commander and staff of the Combined Fleet, or backing the central Pacific option. In such a situation, there was really little choice for the naval staff's upper echelons. When presented with Yamamoto's statement the head of the plans division noted simply that the staff had best try to accommodate Yamamoto's requirements. Subsequently, in presenting a report to his superiors, the principle of *qui tacit consensit* prevailed, with the deputy chief of naval operations nodding his agreement with this assessment and the chief of naval operations making no comment. It was, by any standard, a somewhat unusual way of conducting business on which could depend the outcome of the war.

In play at this stage of proceedings were actually two very separate matters. At one level was the fact that the power of decision was vested in the fleet commander: his nominal superiors in the Naval Ministry, having conceded his October 1941 argument that hostilities had to begin with an attack on the U.S. Pacific Fleet at its base in Pearl Harbor, could not now stand against any demand emanating from the Hashirajima naval base. At the second level was the "can-do" philosophy of armed forces, so often to the forefront in matters of working on the most slender of administrative margins, which in this particular case was overlaid by what many observers have defined as "Victory Disease," which afflicted the Japanese armed services in the immediate aftermath of the easy, contemptuous successes registered throughout Southeast Asia over previous weeks. When these two matters are combined, the logic and sequence of events that resulted in approval of the central Pacific strategy becomes discernible, although in reality the questions that were placed against the assumptions and assertions of the Yamamoto fiat were not to be resolved by their being ignored. The reality was that the 5 April agreement saddled the Kaigun with what was, by the least exacting standard, a highly dubious strategic policy.

WITHIN A MATTER OF DAYS, however, the main element of the central Pacific package was undone. On 4 April, Inoue submitted his command's plans for the southwest Pacific endeavor, complete with a timetable that set the moves against Port Moresby and Tulagi for late May. On the following day, he was informed of major organizational changes that would come into effect on 10 April, and that between 20 April and 10 May his command was to have the services of the fleet carrier *Kaga*, six heavy cruisers, and two destroyer flotillas for the Port Moresby operation. In addition, the light carrier *Shoho*, hitherto confined to ferrying duties, was to be activated for service with Inoue's command. Thus was Inoue informed that his command, instead of opening offensive operations in two months' time with a complete carrier division under his control, was ordered to mount an offensive against Port Moresby and Tulagi in little more than three weeks and without the land-based air formations essential if air superiority was to be secured before amphibious forces were committed south of New Guinea.

Not surprisingly, Inoue's reaction to these arrangements was an angry one. His immediate preoccupation was the scale of air support provided for operations, and in this matter he was upheld by a Rikugun increasingly concerned by the antics of its sister service. The Imperial Army, having signed up to the southwest Pacific option, found the latter postponed in favor of an operation about which it had not been consulted. But if it was obliged to give way, its concerns about the Port Moresby move was another matter. Given the Army's concerns, Inoue's request for the *Hiryu* and *Soryu* from the elite Second Carrier Division rather than the *Kaga* and *Shoho* could not be treated lightly.

Nonetheless, there was no question of Inoue's command being afforded this formation. Its units were the most hard-worked of Japan's carriers, and their need for overhaul in the second half of April had been a major consideration in the allocation of the *Kaga* to Inoue in the first place. Accordingly, on 10 April, Yamamoto ordered the transfer of the *Shokaku* and *Zuikaku*, plus two destroyer divisions, the deployment to be effective from 18 April. This order meant that these carriers, then in the Indian Ocean, could not return to Japan before the Port Moresby operation and would be pressed to complete repairs between that venture and the start of the Midway enterprise.

The casualness with which these arrangements were effected belied their importance. As a result of the decisions of 5 April and over the three weeks as various details were added, the Kaigun committed itself to four operations: securing Port Moresby and Tulagi by 10 May (Operation MO), next the occupation of Nauru and Ocean (Operation RY) by 15 May by forces previously employed in the upper Solomons, and then the main central Pacific endeavor, which was to open with an offensive in the western Aleutians (Operation AL) before the main operation, against Midway (Operation MI), opened on 4 June. The principal forces were to remain in the Midway area, hopefully fighting and winning the decisive battle, until 13 June: thereafter these forces, minus the battleship formations that were to return to Japan, were to make their way to Truk in readiness for the offensive into the southwest Pacific. Leaving aside obvious criticisms that must attach themselves to such a program and schedule, the general plan made the cardinal error of rendering the working of the main operation, against Midway, dependent upon the outcome of a secondary operation, against Port Moresby, which, by definition, was not properly invested: the provision of two carriers to an operation in waters known to be covered by two American carriers gave no margin of superiority.

The detail of the main endeavor, moreover, compounded the error. The Aleutians operation was to open with an attack on the U.S. base at Dutch Harbor on 3 June and then be followed by the occupation of Kiska and Adak on 5 June and Attu on the 12th. But the forces detailed for these operations included the carrier *Junyo*, which carried part of the air group destined for Midway. How she were to operate in the Aleutians and at the same time deliver aircraft to Midway, presumably in time for their playing a full and effective part in the decisive battle, is not exactly clear. But the role of this carrier and her companion, the *Ryujo*, should not obscure the main point. Their absence from the central Pacific would not be important as long as the *Shokaku* and *Zuikaku* were able to be transferred from one operation to another without let or hindrance, but therein was the rub: events conspired to ensure that these two carriers could not take part in Operation MI, and without them the Japanese had no margin of superiority at the point of contact. As it was, these various points of weakness, the product of a strategic and operational confusion that contained the ingredients of defeat, were wholly unsuspected within the Combined Fleet, where, it would seem, overconfidence and self-deception abounded in equal measure.

2

THE AMERICAN SITUATION
AND PLAN OF CAMPAIGN

A ll nations err in the waging of war. Japan made the mistake of assuming that it could set the terms of reference for the war that it initiated in December 1941, and in its devising of plans of campaign for the southwest and central Pacific in 1942 the Kaigun made a second basic error. Its assumption of realizable aims through precise, exact, offensive operations ran directly counter to the fundamental Clausewitzian element in war: chance. War is neither the preserve of the intellect nor is it intrinsically rational or scientific: its operations very seldom follow paths to results that have been foreseen. For its part, the United States was to find that in the Pacific almost two years, and in the European theater more than thirty months, were to pass after its entry into the Second World War before it could make war as it would. Before that time Washington was obliged, for the most part, to make war as it found it.

America's error in misunderstanding the conflict in which it found itself after December 1941 stemmed from the situation that had prevailed after July 1941. The American attempt to deter Japan with inadequate force resulted in a series of defeats that redefined national obligations in the Pacific. Critical in this process was this series of defeats that primarily concerned Britain, with which the United States had divided the Pacific and Southeast Asia into separate areas of responsibility. The southwest Pacific was a British responsibility, but between 14 November and 19 December 1941 British naval losses were more severe than those of the U.S. Navy at Pearl Harbor. The start of the Pacific war left the southwest Pacific, Australia, and New Zealand undefended and, unless the Americans assumed responsibility for their protection, indefensible.

It was not until 17 February 1942 that the Americans formally took on the defense of Australia, although in effect the obligation had been accepted for some weeks before formal acknowledgment. The securing of the line of communications to eastern Australia was part of the process. Before the outbreak of war, American plans provided for garrisons in the Philippines, Hawaii, Alaska, and the Panama Canal Zone, with outposts at Guam, Wake, Johnston, Palmyra, Midway, and eastern Samoa. By the end of March 1942, American planning, in addition to the three major commitments, had assigned major forces to eastern Samoa, Fiji, New Caledonia, and to New Zealand and Australia, with Christmas, Canton, Bora Bora, Efate, and Tongabatu destined to play host to smaller U.S. garrisons. For the Americans the critical point about the opening weeks of the Pacific war was the survival of carriers that necessarily had to divide their attention between the central and southwest Pacific. Their role was primarily defensive. The few offensive missions that were staged amounted to little more than pecking around the rim and were of no great consequence, the Huon Gulf action of 10 March excepted.

In these months, however, there were two developments that came together during April 1942. The first was the appointment of Admiral Ernest J. King as Chief of Naval Operations and Commander-in-Chief U.S. Fleet and Admiral Chester W. Nimitz as Commander-in-Chief Pacific Fleet and Pacific Ocean Areas. Issues of national policy did not depend on any single appointment or appointments, but the fact was that with King and Nimitz the United States had the foundation of the naval team that was to craft the offensive across the Pacific, and both

King and Nimitz sought battle, specifically battle against Japanese carrier forces. The second development was the fact that they possessed the means whereby they could, if they so decided, meet a Japanese carrier threat. This means was access to Japanese naval signals made available through signals intelligence.

THE ORGANIZATION THROUGH which the senior American commanders were to become aware of Japanese plans and intentions was OP-20-G, which was the Communication Security Section of the Office of Naval Communications, specifically through OP-20-GX, which dealt with traffic analysis and direction-finding, and OP-20-GY, which handled cryptanalysis. The former, which after 1937 had a series of listening stations established across the Pacific, had provided warning of the Japanese occupation of southern French Indo-China in July 1941, and in November 1941 the Japanese decision for war had been predicated on the basis of the Kaigun's deployment of forces facing Southeast Asia. The American strength in this field of signals intelligence lay in the fact that work over four years had produced a certain familiarity with the Japanese modus operandi. The weakness was obvious: the contents of the signals that were monitored could not be read.

The Japanese Navy, like all the major combat navies of this war, operated a baffling array of codes and ciphers, all but incomprehensible to the outsider. Roughly one-half of Japanese operational traffic was entrusted to the D, later the RO, code, known to the Americans as JN-25. At the outbreak of war this code, the second version to be encountered, was known as JN-25b. By a process that will always defy the understanding of anyone not involved in such efforts, by the end of March 1942 the Allies had compromised this code to the extent that some 10 to 15 percent of two-fifths of all signals using this code could be read. Overall, some 2 percent of all Japanese signals could be read, but with traffic analysis pointing the way the Americans were basically aware of which signals to ignore and which ones to acknowledge.

During April the allied penetration of JN-25b occurred on a scale that allowed as much as 85 percent of some signals to be read. Complete recovery was extremely rare, but the scheduled, routine change of codes and ciphers by the Kaigun that should have taken place on

1 April was deferred until 1 May and then postponed to 1 June. Such postponement, which broke standard operating procedures, was crucial because had the Japanese made their scheduled change, the Americans would have been denied access to Japanese signals that virtually alone presented the U.S. Navy with advantage at Midway. As it was, on 9 April the Americans took their first significant step on the path that was to lead to the Battle of the Coral Sea: the discovery that the *Kaga* was communicating with Inoue's South Seas Force, an unusual state of affairs that suggested that she might be bound for the southwest Pacific. This was the first indication that the Kaigun might be planning some move beyond Rabaul. It was followed the next day by the Americans buying into the British assessment that six Japanese carriers were presently in the Indian Ocean: the American deduction was that they could not be freed for operations in the southwest Pacific before May.

On 15 April the Americans were able to recover the full text of a signal sent by the Fifth Carrier Division to Inoue in which the latter was informed that the *Shokaku* and *Zuikaku* would leave Formosa for Truk on 28 April. Error led the Americans to believe that the Japanese carrier force would be leaving Truk on 28 April: moreover, they thought that the *Shokaku* and *Zuikaku* had been ordered to join Inoue's command in addition to the *Kaga*. At this stage the Americans had no indication of the extent of Japanese ambitions in this theater. There was a suspicion that their next move would be in the Solomons, but Port Moresby, for want of any real alternative, presented itself as the likely Japanese target. It was not until 30 April that the Solomons-Port Moresby combination could be confirmed.

This detail, however, was lacking on 17 April when Nimitz met with his staff to consider how to meet the Japanese challenge in the southwest Pacific. With three of four American carriers in the Pacific committed to the Doolittle Raid, only one carrier remained in the southwest Pacific, and alone the *Yorktown* could neither deter nor defeat a Japanese move in this theater. After 18 April the *Hornet* and *Enterprise* headed back to Hawaii, thereby freeing the *Lexington* to return to the southwest Pacific. The subsequent frenzy of Japanese naval and air activity after the Doolittle Raid meant that any move in the southwest Pacific had to be delayed until the first week of May.

The American decision to contest the next Japanese move in the southwest Pacific emerged from a series of Pacific Fleet staff meetings between 20 and 22 April. At this stage the Americans expected the Japanese to move with perhaps five carriers, two battleships, about five heavy cruisers, light forces, and the equivalent of an Army division against both Port Moresby and the Solomons. The decision to contest the next Japanese moves with a force that could not number more than two carriers would thus appear somewhat foolhardy, but the Pacific

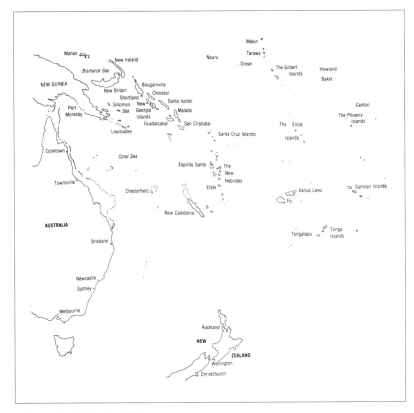

THE SOUTHWEST PACIFIC

From H. P. Willmott, *The Barrier and the Javelin: Japanese and Allied Pacific Strategies, February to June 1942* (Annapolis: Naval Institute Press, 1983), 125.

Fleet, with a low opinion of Japanese fighting worth, could hardly decline the chance of battle. On the assumption that the central Pacific would remain quiet, it was prepared to deploy all four of its carriers to the southwest Pacific during May in order to break the enemy offensive. American planning indicated that the *Enterprise* and *Hornet* would be able to join the *Lexington* and *Yorktown* in theater between

14 and 16 May, although by the time this conclusion was reached, the thinking at Pearl Harbor was that their arrival in the southwest Pacific would result in the relief of the *Yorktown*.

The Pacific Fleet's thinking and proposals had to be approved by superior authority, and such approval was forthcoming at meetings between King and Nimitz in San Francisco held from 25 to 27 April. Ease of agreement belied difficulty of decision. At issue were two matters. The decision to give battle in defense of Port Moresby necessarily involved giving battle on the basis of numerical inferiority, and the decision to commit carrier formations to the southwest Pacific reversed the whole thrust of American national policy since the outbreak of the war. The central Pacific had been seen as the top priority in the Pacific. Now, in April 1942, the decision to seek battle in defense of Port Moresby involved the full offensive power of the U.S. Pacific Fleet concentrated some 3,000 miles from Pearl Harbor. But against this fact was one simple reality: the Japanese were writing the script, and in so doing they provided support for King in his dealings with the real enemy—the U.S. Army, whether in the form of General George C. Marshall, Chief of Staff, in Washington, or General Douglas A. MacArthur, Supreme Allied Commander, South West Pacific Command.

Thus far in the war the Navy had been successful in arguing its case and priorities. The United States entered the war with a "Germany-first" strategy, but virtually all the American commitments in the first five months of war were to the Pacific, not the European theater of operations. By the time that the Navy put together the main features of the plan to meet an enemy challenge in the southwest Pacific, the Army's view was hardening against further commitments in the Pacific. To Marshall, the forces already in or earmarked for the Pacific would have to be sufficient for the moment. The problem for Marshall was MacArthur's insistence that his theater be made the theater of operations in the Pacific, but King and Nimitz had no such problem with MacArthur's delusions of grandeur and self-importance. The San Francisco meetings were held in the week after the South West Pacific Command came into existence, and it was somewhat unfortunate that the decision to fight in defense of Port Moresby necessarily involved naval formations operating in this command's area of responsibility. For King and Nimitz, however, there was no real difficulty; MacArthur and his command were simply ignored.

Nimitz issued the instructions that were to result in the Battle of the Coral Sea on 29 April. In the time between the staff meetings in Pearl Harbor and the San Francisco meetings, signals intelligence had been able to deduce most of the elements that made up Japanese intentions. The twin objectives of Port Moresby and the Solomons were identified, as were subsequent operations against Nauru and Ocean. Only in one matter did the Americans still labor under misapprehension: as late as 1 May, Pacific Fleet intelligence had not detected any indication of a major Japanese effort in the central Pacific.

THE MAIN FEATURES of Nimitz's plan was for Task Force 17, under the command of Rear Admiral Frank J. Fletcher with the *Yorktown*, three heavy cruisers, and four destroyers plus a replenishment group of two oilers and two destroyers, to effect a rendezvous with Task Force 11, consisting of the carrier *Lexington*, two heavy cruisers, and five destroyers, in the eastern Coral Sea. With various American and Australian units already in the area, Fletcher was empowered, as overall commander of carrier forces, to "have discretion to take action to intercept the enemy and keep open vital lines of communication between the United States and Australia."* Fletcher was to hand over command to Vice Admiral William F. Halsey when the latter arrived in theater with Task Force 16. Halsey was to be under orders to "check further advance of the enemy in the New Guinea-Solomons by destroying enemy ships, shipping, and aircraft." Depending on the situation, Halsey would be allowed to retain the carrier forces already in theater, but in accordance with King's general instructions about observing a balance of forces between the southwest and central Pacific sectors, the *Yorktown* was tentatively earmarked for a return to Pearl Harbor on or about 15 May, the *Lexington* on 1 June.

With land-based aircraft, flying boats, and submarines also added to the Allied order of battle, Fletcher's general intention was to take up a position east of the Louisades and between Rennell Island and Guadalcanal, hopefully clear of Japanese reconnaissance aircraft but in a position to strike at Japanese forces moving through the northern

---

*Bernard A. Millot, *The Battle of the Coral Sea* (London: Allan, 1974), 35.

Coral Sea against Port Moresby. The only threat to this intention was the Japanese plan to secure Tulagi and operate flying boats from there over the very waters in which Fletcher and the American carriers were to lurk, hence the need to destroy the Japanese units thus dedicated at the outset.

Leaving aside the details of the Battle of the Coral Sea until Chapter 3, perhaps the most relevant observation that can be made about the American plan is how similar it was to Operation MI, in that with no assured margin of superiority both sides sought a central position from which to strike in turn at separated enemy formations. Where plans differed was the element of risk—in the Japanese case discounted from consideration, in the American case definitely calculated as a result of detailed knowledge of the enemy's order of battle and plan of campaign. The critical point was that the Americans had an advantage of timing and could begin proceedings with basic equality in the air and superiority of numbers of warships at the point of contact. Indeed, at the Coral Sea this American advantage was magnified by the fact that the Japanese had picked up radio traffic that heralded the Doolittle Raid as early as 10 April and had anticipated American intentions correctly. The Japanese therefore assumed that the Americans would not be able to deploy two carriers in the southwest Pacific in advance of Operation MO. The Japanese calculation was correct because the carriers that had been used for the Doolittle Raid could not be redeployed to the southwest Pacific before the Japanese moves unfolded. Tokyo's error lay in an underestimation of American overall carrier numbers in the Pacific and King's willingness to finesse the central Pacific requirement in order to have a carrier force in the southwest Pacific.

THE FIRST REAL CAUSE for American reconsideration of enemy objectives was presented by the Battle of the Coral Sea. After both the initial exchanges and then the main carrier battle, Allied intelligence failed to detect any sign of Japanese forces moving quickly or en masse to the southwest Pacific, as would have been the case if priority was afforded that area. The absence of any major movement of forces gave cause for thought, and no less important was a double realization that impressed itself upon American consciousness just before the start of this battle.

On or about 4 May it suddenly occurred to the authorities at Pearl Harbor that the only Japanese units in the southwest Pacific theater were those assigned to Operation MO, and that for the first time since the outbreak of hostilities the Combined Fleet, other than the forces assigned to Operation MO, was gathered in home waters.

The American high command remained committed to the southwest Pacific thesis throughout the first nine or ten days of May 1942, but Pearl Harbor sources on 9 May suggested that the assumption of the importance of the southwest Pacific in Japanese calculations may have been overstated and that their next move need not come in this theater. In fact, on 6 May these same sources had acknowledged that the Japanese could strike against the Aleutians and in the central sector, and on the 11th the decoding station at Melbourne identified Guam and Saipan as areas of enemy concentration for forthcoming operations. Having also recovered a signal on 5 May asking for additional refueling hose, the Americans were slowly becoming aware that some major long-range operation was in hand. The problem for the Americans, however, was that there was no clear indication of where the enemy's next blow might fall. The partial recovery of a signal from the carrier force to the authorities at Truk requesting berthing assignments for ships arriving there on or about 20 June did not ease matters since it invited the conclusion that Japanese forces would arrive in Truk in anticipation of this main-force undertaking rather than after it had been conducted. But indications that the Japanese intended to occupy Nauru and Ocean after the Port Moresby effort suggested that the southwest Pacific theater was not at the heart of Tokyo's calculations. The Japanese would hardly bother with these islands at this particular time if their main offensive effort was to be made in this theater: the only reason for operations to secure these islands was Japanese identification of priorities outside the southwest Pacific.

By the end of the second week of May, therefore, American naval authorities were in the process of reconsidering basic assumptions, and indeed by mid-May 1942 they had come to believe that the next Japanese move was likely to be in the central Pacific. There were, however, three sets of problems with this conclusion. The first, very simply, was that in the immediate aftermath of the Coral Sea battle, King found himself involved in a major argument with Marshall and General Henry H. "Hap" Arnold over theater allocations and was committed fully to the southwest Pacific thesis. Marshall sought to halt further deployment of military and army air formations into the southwest Pacific, his argument being that the Germany-first priority could not survive the continued drain of resources into the southwest Pacific. To King the defensive requirement of the southwest Pacific theater was primarily determined by the scale and immediacy of the threat to which it was subjected, and he had no confidence in land-based army air formations being shuffled around within the theater. His immediate concern was that he could not abandon the southwest Pacific in the middle of a major interservice argument despite the fact that the southwest Pacific thesis and priority were in the process of being discarded even as the argument in Washington unfolded.

The second problem was that even as the Americans considered the evidence and concluded that the Japanese were likely to undertake major offensive action between 1 and 5 June, there was no clear indication of where in the central Pacific their effort would be made. Whether the Japanese would move against Pearl Harbor, or against both Midway and Pearl Harbor, or against first Midway and then Pearl Harbor, eluded the Americans until the end of the third week of May. Aware that the Japanese were referring to their central Pacific priority as AF and with strong supporting evidence to suggest that AG was Pearl Harbor and AF was Midway, the American intelligence team at Pearl Harbor prised the crucial information from the enemy. Sending a message by cable to the Midway garrison instructing it to transmit a signal in clear to the effect that the water purification system on the atoll had broken down, the Americans hoped that the signal would be intercepted by Japanese listening stations and would be reported to superior authority in a code that had been broken. So it happened to the extent that the Combined Fleet gave orders for a water carrier to be added to the forces bound for Midway, and the American interception of the Wake station's signal ended all doubts about Japanese priorities.

The third problem was that of incredulity. In the days before enemy intentions were laid bare, the question that naturally impressed itself on the American high command was whether the Japanese seriously considered using virtually the whole of the Combined Fleet to secure two or three desolate islands in the Aleutians and one atoll in the central Pacific. Inevitably, the very scale of Japanese preparations and sheer volume of radio traffic provided the answer to the question: their reliance on radio was confirmation of necessity, not a hoax.

The unraveling of the Japanese plan of campaign largely came about between 20 and 24 May, and the timing was ironic in a double sense. First, on 24 May the Japanese changed their major codes and ciphers. The Americans knew on this day that, other than detail with respect to signals that had not been fully recovered, their access to Japanese signals would be nonexistent for several months, but by this stage such a consideration was not overly important. The second point was not so obvious to either side, but around the middle of the month, with the *Enterprise* and *Hornet* in the southwest Pacific and deliberately revealing their presence to deflect the Japanese from the occupation of Nauru and Ocean, the Japanese had a fleeting opportunity to effect Operation MI. In all likelihood they could have done so easily in exactly the way that their plans foretold. Japanese formations, whether in home waters or in the Marianas, were closer to Midway than the American carriers at Noumea, which was 3,954 miles from Oahu. Apart from the fact that logistical and other administrative considerations ensured that the Japanese could not make their move against Midway until the first week of June 1942, it is ironic that criticism of Yamamoto for not delaying the Midway operation in order to wait for the *Zuikaku* or both the *Shokaku* and *Zuikaku* could be countered by the argument that the real criticism of his intention, plan, and schedule was slowness. It may well be that this was the real cost of the sortie into the Indian Ocean in April 1942.

BE THAT AS IT MAY, the basic point was that in the fourth week of May the American intelligence sources at Pearl Harbor laid bare virtually the whole detail of the Japanese plan of campaign, made available by Yamamoto on 20 May in the form of a comprehensive order to all units engaged in Operations AL and MI. The American recovery of the plan was completed on 24 May except for the crucial date-time group (DTG), which was recovered on the 27th. By then, however, most of the American preparations to meet the Japanese moves had been ordered or put into effect, and the recovery of the elusive DTG only confirmed timings that had already been deduced from other sources.

The American reaction to Tokyo's intent, as revealed in the gradual recovery of Japanese signals, manifested itself at different levels and times. The seven old battleships of Task Force 1 were to be kept at San Francisco. With regard to the Aleutians, Nimitz was inclined initially to let them make do with what was already in position. But Alaska was American national territory, and King instructed Nimitz on 17 May to provide a task force for the defense of the Aleutians. By declaring the Aleutians threatened by an enemy fleet, the U.S. Navy secured command and responsibility for the whole Alaskan theater, but this fact did not much alter numbers and deployment of American forces in theater. The number of American bases in the Aleutians were very few and could not be reinforced on any significant scale in what little time remained once Japanese ambitions in the Aleutians were discerned.

Less obviously, the commander sent from Pearl Harbor on 22 May in the destroyer *Reid*, Rear Admiral Robert A. Theobald, was informed on 28 May only that the Japanese planned to descend on Attu, Kiska, and Adak. Neither the source nor the reliability of this information was communicated to Theobald, and as a consequence he did not hesitate to ignore it. With very good reason, Theobald refused to believe that the Japanese actually would seek to secure such worthless real estate as islands in the western and central Aleutians. He thought that the Japanese move into the western Pacific would be a feint, designed to draw American forces westward while the main effort was made either against Dutch Harbor or targets farther to the east. Thus, in spite of orders issued on 30 May to take his task force to a position some 200 miles south of the western Aleutians, Theobald took his formation to a position some 400 miles to the south of Kodiak. The land and air commanders, who apparently shared Theobald's skepticism, held the greater part of their forces in the Anchorage area, in theory beyond the reach of any opening Japanese attack but in positions from which they could move forward to counter enemy moves.

Theobald, in fact, had four naval formations under his command. The first, consisting of six of the old *S*-class submarines, was assigned local reconnaissance duties west of Cold Bay and off the Umnak Passage. To provide direct support to Dutch Harbor and Cold Bay, nine destroyers were deployed at Makushin Bay, on the northern coast of Unalaska, although only six units of Task Group 8.4 were on station on 2 June. To cover the approaches to the islands of the Aleutian chain were twenty assorted units that together comprised Task Group 8.2. Nine of these units were stationed in the Bering Sea, four to the east of St. Paul and the remainder between St. Paul and Atka. The other eleven were deployed in an arc between the southwest and southeast of Dutch Harbor at a range of 200 miles from that base. Supposedly these units were to be spaced at thirty-mile intervals and were to maintain stationary patrol. The force under Theobald's personal command, Task Group 8.6, consisted of two heavy and three light cruisers, five destroyers, and one oiler. This formation was to assemble on the morning of 3 June with units coming from as far afield as Kodiak, San Francisco, Midway, and Pearl Harbor. One destroyer failed to effect the rendezvous and proceeded to Kodiak, arriving on 6 June.

The local defense arrangements of the western Hawaiian islands involved the despatch of single patrol boats to Kure and Midway and single converted tuna boats to Necker, Gardner Pinnacles, Laysan, and Lisanski. Three units were despatched to Pearl Harbor and Hermes Reef, while a destroyer and two seaplane tenders were placed under orders to proceed to French Frigate Shoals. This latter deployment was partly intended to deny the Japanese use of the Shoals for their proposed reconnaissance of Pearl Harbor, and partly the result of the calculation that with extra Catalinas deployed to Midway the Shoals alone offered a place to refuel once battle was joined. On Midway itself the single battalion and Catalina squadron that had been present since the outbreak of war had been steadily reinforced as the means to maintain a larger garrison and air group were developed. In the period immediately before the battle, the number of aircraft, seaplanes, and amphibians on the atoll varied on a daily basis. Of the 121 aircraft on Midway when battle was joined on 4 June, four were B-26 Marauders and seventeen were B-17 Flying Fortresses from the Seventh Air Force, six TBF Avenger torpedo-bombers, fourteen Catalina flying boats and sixteen Catalina amphibians from the Navy, and sixty-four aircraft of various types from the Marine Corps. The latter, however, had been reduced by cannibalization to a total of fifty-four units, and consisted of seventeen TBD-1 Devastators, twelve Vindicators, eighteen F2A Buffaloes, and seven F4F Wildcats.

Nominally available to cover Midway were no fewer than forty-eight submarines. Of this total eight were at Perth in Western Australia with another eleven on patrols from Perth that were scheduled to end at Pearl Harbor: at sea there were four submarines from Pearl Harbor on patrols that were to end at Perth. Of the remaining twenty-five boats, which were all based at Pearl Harbor, eleven were on patrol, and considerations of time and distance meant that units at Pearl Harbor or at sea would have to be despatched to Midway by mid-May if they were to be on station in readiness for the Japanese assault on the atoll. Accordingly, American submarines were organized into three formations. The first, Task Group 7.1, consisted of twelve units with one directed to a position 700 miles due west of Midway where American intelligence believed Japanese forces would rendezvous. Three were instructed to deploy on the arc 250 to 310 degrees at a range of 200 miles from Midway, six on the arc 240 to 360 degrees at a range of 150 miles, and the remaining two were assigned patrol stations on bearings of 310 and 350 degrees from Midway at a range of fifty miles. The second, Task Group 7.2, consisted of three submarines deployed to the east of Midway at a range of 425 miles and in positions from which they could go forward to support Task Group 7.1 or cover the withdrawal of the carrier force. The third, Task Group 7.3, consisted of three submarines—originally four—deployed some 300 miles to the north of Pearl Harbor to guard against the possibility of a diversionary raid on the Pacific Fleet's main base. Six boats at sea but not ordered to the defense of Midway were diverted with orders to search for and attack Japanese units during the withdrawal after the battle. Although a couple of contacts were made, none of the submarines thus directed was able to conduct an attack on any Japanese warship.

THESE VARIOUS MEASURES, important though they were, clearly belonged to the "nice-to-have" classification, and in the final analysis the deployment that really counted, the "need-to-have," involved the carriers. Herein was the immediate American problem because, with the *Saratoga* still on the West Coast, the Americans could rely only on two carriers, the *Enterprise* and *Hornet*. Given that the Japanese were certain to deploy four, possibly five, carriers with the main forces off Midway, two represented an inadequate force with which to give battle. With the Battle of the Coral Sea having made the Americans painfully aware that enemy carrier forces were not to be underestimated, they had to have a third, the *Yorktown*, in order to challenge the Japanese. The basic issue that ultimately governed all American considerations in preparing for Midway was this question of carrier numbers. Given the fact that U.S. carrier air groups were larger than those of their opposite numbers, the Americans could hope to offer battle on the basis of three carriers, but no fewer. Herein is one of the great heroic myths about this battle, namely, the readying of the *Yorktown* in three days despite the estimate that she needed a ninety-day overhaul after Coral Sea.

Task Force 16, with the *Enterprise* and *Hornet*, was ordered to proceed to Pearl Harbor from the southwest Pacific on 16 May and arrived safely on the 26th. Thus, Nimitz had the main part of the force with which to confront the Japanese, but the critical question was the state of the *Yorktown*. After Coral Sea he had been warned that she needed a ninety-day refit to make good her damage, and this assessment seems to have been accurate, but to the wrong question: the right question was how long she would need to be made ready to go to sea and to give battle. The fact that the *Yorktown* had recovered aircraft from the *Lexington* and continued to operate her own group after she had been hit, plus the fact that she withdrew from the battle and then made her way to Pearl Harbor under her own power, pointed to the fact that she could continue to fight, the obvious risk relating to her structural strength and internal integrity being accepted. The problem with the *Yorktown* was not her capacity to give battle but rather what might happen if she incurred further damage without having been able to attend to the damage inflicted in the Coral Sea. To Nimitz on 27 May, when the *Yorktown* entered dry dock, this was a risk that had to be accepted, and in truth there was no real alternative. The *Yorktown* had to be made fit for battle, and she could have her full refit thereafter.

Accordingly, the American order of battle was completed. Task Force 16, in Halsey's absence under the command of Rear Admiral Raymond A. Spruance, sailed from Pearl Harbor on 28 May with the *Enterprise* and *Hornet* (both with seventy-nine aircraft), five heavy cruisers, one light cruiser, and nine destroyers. In company were the two oilers and two more destroyers assigned to their protection. The destroyer *Gain*, having arrived at Pearl Harbor before Task Force 16, was ordered to complete a high-speed run with reinforcements for Midway. She left Pearl Harbor on 23 May and returned on 1 June, and thereby missed being in the carrier screen at Midway as had been intended.

The *Yorktown* was floated from her dry dock shortly before noon on 29 May and lay in the roads while work continued on her for another day. It was on the 30th, therefore, that she began to move under her own power after major repair and replenishment, the latter being no small matter in light of the fact that before going into dockyard hands she had been 101 days at sea. Once under way, the *Yorktown* embarked an air group that numbered fourteen Devastators, eighteen bombers, nineteen scouts, and twenty-seven fighters, two of the Wildcats being lost in an accident on the flight deck. The *Yorktown* was escorted by two heavy cruisers and five destroyers, and this force refueled from the oilers on 1 June before conducting its rendezvous with Task Force 16 in latitude 32 degrees North, longitude 173 degrees West on 2 June.

THE EXAMINATION OF THE PROCESS whereby Japanese signals were compromised, American decisions were reached, and the detail of the subsequent U.S. deployment of forces in readiness for battle is now complete, except for three matters. The first relates to the southwest Pacific theater, and the fact that the various deployments ordered by King and Nimitz left this area in a state that would have been its permanent condition had Marshall secured his way in terms of force allocation. The critical decision to return Task Force 16 to the central Pacific left MacArthur's South West Pacific Command with responsibility for the approaches to Australia, and with more American aircraft in Australia than in any other single Pacific command Nimitz sought to get the Army command to help secure New Caledonia and Samoa. MacArthur, however, refused to have anything to do with the Navy's request.

The second matter concerns one of the little-known aspects of the Battle of Midway. As noted earlier, the Japanese, by virtue of traffic analysis, discerned the Doolittle attack in April 1942. In May the Americans left a seaplane tender and a heavy cruiser in the southwest Pacific to simulate a carrier task group's operations, but the Combined Fleet signals staff detected the buildup of air activity at Pearl Harbor on 30 May and correctly interpreted it to indicate the departure of a carrier force. But Yamamoto's decision to proceed to sea meant that this critical piece of intelligence, tantamount to a warning that an enemy carrier force could well be in the Midway area, could not be passed to

Vice Admiral Nagumo Chuichi's First Carrier Striking Force because of the need to observe radio silence.

The third matter concerns the meeting held by Nimitz, Fletcher, Spruance, and their staffs on the evening of 27 May. When considering the battle overall, one cannot be blind to the fact that on the morning of 4 June events unfolded in a manner that favored the Americans outrageously. It is hard to think how events could have conspired to their better advantage—and it is all the more important to remember that luck was in no small measure earned. At the meeting of 27 May the basic plan took shape with American carrier forces detailed to stand to the northeast of Midway as the Japanese advanced on the atoll from the northwest. The American plan was for their carriers to advance to contact as the Japanese attacked Midway and, relying on accurate reconnaissance reports from Midway's patrolling aircraft, to strike at the Japanese carriers when the latter were committed to operations against Midway and hence minus a considerable part of their air strength. In the course of this meeting, the carrier commanders and staff were brought to the realization that there was a chance, perhaps even a good chance, of their being able to catch the enemy in the process of recovering his aircraft after the strike on Midway.

Through careful attention to detail and calculation of the odds, therefore, the Americans had placed themselves in a position of potential advantage. Overall the balance of forces favored them, and the various weaknesses within the Japanese plan of campaign added to this advantage. The Americans knew the enemy's order of battle, timetable, and plans and had glimpsed an opportunity that might present itself. As the U.S. carrier forces gathered off Point Luck on 2 June, the question that remained over the following days was whether the Americans would secure victory because of their efforts and advantages or whether the Japanese would prevail despite the weaknesses of their plan.

3

THE BATTLE OF THE CORAL SEA

5–8 May 1942

The Battle of the Coral Sea, fought between 5 and 8 May 1942, was both complete in its own right and the overture to Midway in June. The first engagement in which fleet units never sighted one another, it was the first fleet action since the Battle of Jutland (31 May–1 June 1916), with which it is usually contrasted on account of Jutland's being the last in a line of battles that reached back to the Age of Sail. In reality, Jutland and the Coral Sea share numerous points of similarity, and indeed there is more similarity than difference between these two actions.

Both battles were fought with weapons untested in combat. All sides faced unknown dangers without any body of experience and combat knowledge on which to draw. Moreover, they had to contend with uncertain and poor communications in situations in which the area of battle had grown far beyond that prescribed by past experience but in which speeds had increased to an even greater extent, thereby compressing decision-making time. Intelligence ranged between scarce and abundant, but, irrespective of quality, it was invariably misapplied and its full value went unrealized. In both battles what may be termed "target identification" and "fire distribution" were more often wrong than right, and in both actions there were probably as many bad decisions as good ones on the part of commanders who, for a variety of reasons, had only incomplete knowledge of what was happening around them and where the enemy might be. In both actions light, wind, sun, and, above all, night played important roles, and in both actions defensive concerns—the safety of costly ships—were important in helping to ensure what seemed at the time to be an indecisive outcome. In fact, in both battles the defense prevailed and decisively so, in part because of an intelligence advantage that enabled their fighting the battle that accorded with their strategic interest.

THE PRELUDE TO BATTLE was the arrival of Japanese forces at Shortland and the establishment of a seaplane station, with five Mavis flying boats, on 28 April. Then followed the landings at Thousand Ships Bay, Santa Isabel Island, on 2 May and at Tulagi and Gavutu on the morning of 3 May, the resident Australian garrison having evacuated Tanambogo Island on the previous day. The Japanese landings at Tulagi were covered by aircraft from the *Shoho*, which was some 180 miles to the west at dawn on the 3d. By noon she, and other covering forces, had turned back toward the central Solomon Sea in order to be in position to support amphibious forces during the next phase of Operation MO.

Thus far, Japanese plans had been realized without difficulty, but there were two problems in the offing. First, on 1 May the carrier force, commanded by Vice Admiral Takagi Takeo, sailed from Truk; and on the 2d, during its run to the south, it was to fly nine Zekes to Rabaul. On the 2d, however, the Zekes had to return to the carriers after bad weather prevented their reaching Vunakanau airfield. On the following day events repeated themselves, one Zeke being lost. This failure to fly fighters to Rabaul presented a problem disproportionate to the numbers involved. From the start of hostilities the Japanese chose to advance with transports and amphibious forces into waters already controlled by their air power. Now, in May, they chose to abide by past practice—that is, the Japanese had to win air superiority over Port Moresby, a task that had to be achieved by land-based air formations. But the latter had to fight Allied air formations at Port Moresby and in northern Australia, and this was an unequal battle that they could not win.

The slenderness of the margins on which the Japanese were working can be gauged by the fact that on 4 May there were only twelve Zekes at Rabaul and six at Lae from the total of thirty-two that had been available on 25 April. In such a situation the nine Zekes ferried by the carriers seemed very important, but in reality Japanese needs were on the order of nine squadrons, not nine aircraft. The failure to fly off the Zekes successfully on the 2d and 3d thus offered the choice between pressing southward to cover the seaplane bases in the Solomons, or marking time, refueling, and then making another attempt to get the Zekes to Rabaul before proceeding south. In reality, the Japanese needed either to undertake a massive reinforcement of Rabaul to overwhelm Allied aircraft over Port Moresby or to commit the full carrier force against the airfields of northern Australia. In the event the Japanese did neither, and Takagi on 3 May was ordered to commit his air groups to the battle over Port Moresby on the 7th or 8th. With just forty-six Zekes embarked (and this total included the eight so reluctant to depart), such orders represented a dangerous widening of his carriers' responsibilities. The groups from the *Shokaku* and *Zuikaku* were to cover the positions in the lower Solomons, provide distant cover for amphibious forces bound for Port Moresby, supply the bulk of the fighters that would have to fight and win the battle for air supremacy over eastern New Guinea, and fight and win any battle that might result from the arrival of an enemy task force on the scene. And herein was the second of the two problems that were in the offing, and which was quite unknown to the Japanese at this stage: American carrier formations were already in theater and inside the reconnaissance line that Japanese submarines were supposed to establish. With the Japanese carriers off Rabaul the bases in the lower Solomons were unsupported, and the *Yorktown* was in a position to strike at Tulagi before the Japanese carriers could come on station.

The real Japanese problem, however, was that the operational timetable was so tight that there could be no delay in any single part of Operation MO. Thus, while the carriers fell behind schedule coming south from Truk, there was no question of the Japanese postponing the main phase of operations: the units tasked to establish a seaplane base in the Deboyne Islands sailed from Rabaul on 3 May as planned, while the transports and attack formations bound for Port Moresby sailed the follow day. In this situation, the Americans were in a position to repeat the March success in Huon Gulf, but the difficulties that Task Force 11 experienced in trying to refuel on the 3d meant that only one carrier, the *Yorktown*, was able to strike at bases in the Solomons, and she never received warning of the Japanese presence at Tulagi until late on the 3d, by which time most of the units that had been involved in the occupation of Tulagi had dispersed.

When word did arrive in the *Yorktown* of the Japanese presence in the lower Solomons, she and her escorts turned north and worked up to 27 knots to be in a position to strike at Tulagi at dawn. On the 4th the *Yorktown* launched no fewer than four attacks on shipping at Tulagi and accounted for one destroyer-transport, three small auxiliary minesweepers, four landing barges, and five Mavis flying boats. Even though the Americans believed that more units had been sunk, there was no escaping the conclusion that results were "disappointingly meagre."* No less important, the Japanese had been made aware that an American carrier force was in theater. When the *Yorktown* recovered the last of her attacking aircraft, Task Force 17 settled on a course to the south, clear of the immediate search areas.

On the following morning TF 17 effected a rendezvous with Task Force 11 in latitude 15 degrees South, longitude 160 degrees East. With units of Task Force 44 also in company, the concentrated Allied force was some 320 miles south of Guadalcanal. In this position, away from the general direction of enemy movement and in a reconnaissance blind spot, TF 17 set about refueling. At this stage the advantage clearly lay with the Americans, the Japanese being forced to react to events and clearly surprised that battle had begun days before schedule. But as 5 May passed with no contact between enemy formations, the advantage that the Americans had enjoyed over the previous days slowly began to shift in allegiance, and on two counts. First, on 4 May the Americans had been able to conduct their strikes on Tulagi from be-

*Dudley McCarthy, *Australia in the War of 1939–1945*, Series 1, *Army. The Southwest Pacific Area: First Year. Kakoda to Wau* (Canberra: Australian War Memorial, 1959), 5:80.

neath the cover provided by a cold front that had established itself across the Solomon Sea: by the following day, with its position all but unchanged, the American carriers were clear of the front. Second, as attention focused on the Solomon Sea and the Louisades, these carriers would have to come westward to positions from which to attack Japanese formations moving on Port Moresby. In so doing they would

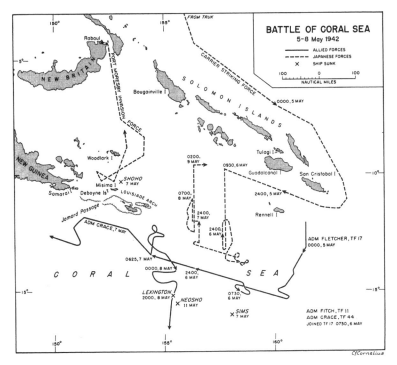

BATTLE OF THE CORAL SEA, 5–8 MAY 1942

From Samuel Milner, *The War in the Pacific: Victory in Papua* (Washington, DC: Center of Military History, U.S. Army, 1957), 35.

place themselves where Japanese reconnaissance aircraft were certain to search as the Japanese carrier force came around the lower Solomons and into a position to cover the assault shipping north of the Louisades.

The Japanese carrier force was in the process of refueling during the morning of 4 May, and by the vagaries of the radio net did not detect what was happening at Tulagi. It was not until the afternoon that it received orders from Inoue to make up lost time. This was not possible: an extended high-speed chase around the lower Solomons necessarily would involve more refueling and having to await the arrival of the oiler. As a result it was not until noon on the 5th that the Japanese carriers entered the eastern Coral Sea and faced a problem that might have been prevented. During the morning, Inoue, when presented with a choice between searching the Solomon and Coral Seas for enemy carriers and continuing the air offensive against Port Moresby, opted for the latter. As a result, the Japanese carrier force lacked any support in seeking to ascertain the whereabouts of its enemy. This was far more significant than might appear. Japanese carrier doctrine held to the view that aircraft assigned reconnaissance duties represented offensive power wasted: scouting duties were the responsibility of seaplanes. The problem for the *Shokaku* and *Zuikaku* was that the seaplane-cruisers were in home waters. In these circumstances, on both this and the following day the Japanese and American carrier formations were acutely aware of the delicacy of their respective positions. The Americans ran the risk of being caught by the Japanese carriers as they moved against shipping between Rabaul and the Jomard Passage while the Japanese carriers were no less aware that they could be caught by a flank attack. The more obvious danger, however, was that the enemy might savage the assault shipping bound for Port Moresby, the safety of which had to be the Japanese priority.

PERHAPS THE STRANGEST ASPECT of the Battle of the Coral Sea was the simple fact that American and Japanese carriers were in the Coral Sea for the best part of three days before they traded blows. Such lack of contact was certainly not the result of lack of trying, most obviously on 7 May. Indeed, on 6 May the failure of the carrier formations to find one another was remarkable given that on occasion they were separated by only some seventy miles, but the fact that contact proved elusive on the 6th ensured that contact was certain to be made on the 7th as time and space shrank. With Japanese amphibious and assault forces approaching the Louisades, the gathering in the Solomon Sea was certain to be observed and reported by Allied land-based aircraft, amphibians, or carrier-based aircraft. At the same time the Japanese failure to find an enemy carrier force on the 6th led to the decision to commit a dozen Kates to a search to the south and east.

Inevitably, in the first hours of daylight on 7 May there were a number of contacts and reports made, and perhaps equally inevitably the reports that drew action were the ones that contained the worst errors. In the event, however, the Americans commanded the better fortune because the various errors of reporting more or less resolved themselves and left them free to attack and sink the *Shoho* while remaining clear of the attentions of the *Shokaku* and *Zuikaku*. The *Shoho*, with no armor and minimal subdivision into compartments, was very literally torn apart by perhaps as many as thirteen bombs and seven torpedoes. She had just two fighters in her combat air patrol, and the four heavy cruisers in company left her to face three successive attacks without support. When she sank, the same cruisers left the scene without attempting to recover any of the crew from the water.

At the same time as American carrier aircraft fell upon the *Shoho*, sixty Kates and Vals, with eighteen Zekes, were directed against two units that had been reported as an enemy carrier and cruiser but instead were the oiler *Neosho* and destroyer *Sims*. The latter was peremptorily despatched, the *Neosho* less easily since she survived for four days before sinking. The point, however, is that when the Japanese aircraft arrived over their targets only to find ships very different from what they had been led to expect, they wasted valuable time searching for their real enemy before returning to deal with what was there. With the Japanese critically being an hour or two behind the Americans in the launching and hence recovery of their aircraft, their carriers, belatedly given the correct position of their American opposite numbers, were left in a position of potentially great vulnerability, especially because the American carriers, having eliminated the *Shoho*, knew from the attack on the *Sims* and *Neosho* that their enemy was to the east. The American carriers were able to muster aircraft for a second strike mission some two hours before the Japanese carriers, but without any clear indication of the enemy's whereabouts and with sunset at about 1815, Fletcher decided against attempting a strike. The Japanese had no such inhibitions, and at 1615 they flew off fifteen Kates and a dozen Vals to find and attack the Americans.

Ordered to search, find, and attack an enemy formation some 280 miles to the west of their carriers, the Japanese aircraft were forced off course by appalling weather and searched beyond the American

carrier force, which was some 150 miles west of the Japanese formation. Finally despairing of finding the enemy, most of the Japanese aircraft jettisoned their ordnance in an attempt to improve their speed
and range. In seeking to return to their carriers, some fell afoul of
Wildcats from the American combat air patrol that were directed
against them while others, in the failing light, attempted to land on the
American carriers. Overall, the Japanese lost nine aircraft in this one
mission, which closed proceedings on 7 May.

In the hours that remained to 7 May the American and Japanese
carrier formations drew apart as they prepared for an encounter on the
following morning that both sides knew could not be avoided and that
would decide the issue. In one sense, however, the issue had already
been decided because on this day the Japanese had secured the position
of advantage, on the tail of an unsuspecting enemy, and then squan-
dered their opportunity. To compound the failure, the Americans had
accounted for one light carrier and, more important, had forced the
postponement of the whole of the Port Moresby undertaking since
there was no question of the Japanese attempting to cross the line of
the Louisades with a detached Allied cruiser force standing between the
Jomard Passage and Port Moresby and with American carriers standing to the east. What was worse about the Japanese failure on 7 May
was the fact that the numerical balance, in terms of carrier air groups,
worsened to their considerable disadvantage as a result of the losses of
this day: having lost one in seven of their bombers on the 7th, the Japanese carriers on the morning of 8 May had only 109 aircraft, of which
fourteen were nonoperational, compared to the 121 of the American
carriers. In terms of available strike aircraft, the Americans entered
8 May with a very real advantage of eighty-nine Dauntlesses and Devastators compared to the fifty-eight Vals and Kates of the Japanese
carriers.

In addition, the Americans on the morning of 8 May were endowed with two more potentially telling advantages: the greater number of cruisers, destroyers, and guns available to the screening
formations compared to their opposite numbers; and the radar and
homing devices of the *Lexington* and *Yorktown*. Against this threat the
Japanese carriers hugged the cover provided by the cold front. As it was,
with both carrier formations launching reconnaissance missions
around 0600, the two sides found one another at roughly the same
time. The closeness of contact brought about the very situation that

neither side wanted: more or less simultaneous contact meant that neither side could attack without being attacked in turn.

Both sides had to await clarification and confirmation of the initial sighting reports, and it was not until 0900 that the Americans began to launch aircraft for the strike. For their part, the Japanese carriers began to launch their aircraft at 0915. With their slight advantage of time, the Americans were to conduct their attack first, though under circumstances that were very different from what was intended. The flying-off process was uncoordinated, with the result that the *Yorktown*'s group attacked some thirty minutes ahead of the *Lexington*'s aircraft. The *Yorktown*'s dive-bombers found part of the Japanese carrier formation, with just the *Shokaku*, at 1032 but chose to await the arrival of the Devastators in an attempt to mount a coordinated attack. The torpedo-bombers found themselves unable to mount a scissors attack and were able to release their torpedoes only at ranges between 1,000 and 2,000 yards from off the port bow. With the *Shokaku* turning away and avoiding the torpedoes, the Dauntlesses, having wasted twenty-five minutes and now short of fuel, were obliged to attack the same carrier.

The Dauntlesses hit the *Shokaku* with two 1,000-pound bombs. One hit the aircraft engine room and in effect ended the *Shokaku*'s ability to service her aircraft, and the other hit the anchor windlass room and set off a huge avgas (aviation gas) explosion. The Dauntlesses claimed to have left the carrier sinking, but the fact was that the *Shokaku* and *Zuikaku* had armored avgas compartments built into the hull with carbon dioxide in the surrounding voids. The result was that the *Shokaku* contained the explosion and easily brought the resultant fires under control, although with the force of the explosion wrecking the forward part of the flight deck the *Shokaku*'s ability to launch aircraft was ended. Some thirty minutes later four Dauntlesses and eleven Devastators from the *Lexington* arrived on the scene. They found a carrier formation and attacked one seemingly unharmed carrier, claiming to have hit it seven times and leaving it badly damaged. In fact, only one hit was recorded, on the arrester gear of the *Shokaku*. With no continuity in the mounting of these attacks, the American groups had hit just the one carrier twice. Nonetheless, unable to fly off, land, and service her aircraft, the *Shokaku* was eliminated from the battle, and at about 1300, in the company of two heavy cruisers and two destroyers, she turned for Truk and thence for Kure. Her return to home waters proved eventful. By monitoring Japanese radio traffic the Americans tried to put four submarines on interception courses around Truk and then deployed another four on the direct route between Truk and Kure. The *Shokaku* avoided contact with every one of these submarines. She was also fortunate in that near-misses had raised some of her plates; by the time she reached home waters, gradual flooding adversely affected her stability.

While the *Shokaku* was undergoing attack, her aircraft were to play their part in restoring balance to the proceedings. She and the *Zuikaku* flew off eighteen Zekes, eighteen Kates, and thirty-three Vals against the American carriers, retaining just four Vals and nineteen Zekes in reserve. The smallness of the number of fighters retained for the combat air patrol, which was worsened by the fact that the *Shokaku* and *Zuikaku* had become separated in the course of flying operations, helps to explain why the American aircraft suffered relatively light losses—a total of nineteen—in their attacks. For their part, after they had despatched their attack force, the American carriers retained just twenty-five aircraft—eight Wildcats and eight Dauntlesses with the *Yorktown* and nine Wildcats with the *Lexington*—with which to mount the combat air patrol, but these numbers were increased by scouts returning from their reconnaissance mission.

The Japanese aircraft immediately formed up together and moved out to attack the American carriers. As they set out, they met the Kate that had given the original sighting reports of the enemy formation. This plane was returning to her carrier but ensured her own destruction by reversing course and leading the assembled Japanese aircraft to their intended prey. Warned of the Japanese approach by radar, the American formation worked up to 25 knots as the Japanese force broke down into attack formations at 1112. By 1118, American ships were making 30 knots as the Japanese attack began. Under bombardment, and with the *Yorktown* and *Lexington* having different turning circles, the American formation divided, with the *Yorktown* being screened by three heavy cruisers and three destroyers and the *Lexington* by two heavy cruisers and four destroyers.

Exactly which aircraft and ships did battle with one another over the next fourteen minutes has long been the subject of historical dispute, but one aspect of these encounters gives evidence of the difficulty that attends definitive narrative. American after-action reports indicated that twenty-seven Zekes, fifteen Vals, and thirty-one Kates were destroyed on 8 May, with twenty-two of the fighters, eleven of the Vals, and all of the Kates destroyed in the course of this one attack on TF 17. In fact, the Japanese lost one Zeke, thirteen Vals, and eight Kates.

It seems likely that the Japanese offensive began with Kates from the *Zuikaku* attacking the *Lexington* just before Kates from the *Shokaku* attacked the *Yorktown*, these two efforts being made between 1118 and 1121 or thereabouts. The *Yorktown* was then subjected to dive-bombing, probably by Vals from the *Shokaku*, between about 1124 and 1130, while the *Lexington* received similar attention between 1126 and 1132. An attack by a lone Kate on the *Yorktown* at 1140 is generally regarded as having ended proceedings.

The opening torpedo attacks on the American carriers, similar to those that had been made on the *Shokaku*, were launched at ranges of 1,000 to 1,500 yards, which reduced the chances of hits. The *Yorktown*, heeling under a full rudder as she circled to starboard at 32 knots, managed to evade all of the torpedoes aimed at her, but the bigger *Lexington* was struck by two torpedoes in the third and last attack to which she was subjected. Indeed, she was fortunate not to have been struck by more: two torpedoes, running deep, passed under her, and three more torpedoes passed within 200 feet of the ship. A matter of seconds separated the *Lexington* from a series of hits that certainly would have destroyed her at the very outset of this action.

The *Lexington* seemed to absorb the two hits—both to port and forward of the superstructure—with ease. Three of the sixteen boiler rooms had to be closed because of ruptured feeder lines, and the elevators were jammed in the raised position. One of the ship's generator rooms had to be evacuated because the ventilation system stopped working, and the *Lexington* began to list. The Vals registered two hits, and one near-miss, of any importance. All three bombs caused heavy casualties, but they accounted for only one secondary and three tertiary guns and caused minor damage to the flight deck and flooding to three compartments. Overall, the *Lexington* was left with a list of 7 degrees to port but seemed in no danger. Her fighting efficiency had not been impaired to any real extent and her machinery was intact.

The *Yorktown* came through her ordeal with equal facility. She was hit only once, by a bomb that penetrated three decks before exploding in an aviation stores room, with the effects of the blast damaging the pedestal of the radar antenna and intakes to three boiler rooms. One near-miss ruptured a drained fuel duct and a second near-miss

detonated underwater with a mining effect. Perhaps with other near-
misses adding to the damage, the *Yorktown* was perforated over one-
quarter of her length, and with her armor belt buckled she trailed an
oil slick that ultimately reached ten miles behind her. Interestingly, the
Japanese claims proved as exaggerated as those of the Americans. The
Lexington was claimed to have been hit by nine torpedoes and ten
bombs and to have been left sinking; the *Yorktown* was alleged to have
been hit by three torpedoes and eight bombs and left in a heavily damaged state. The odd point about both sets of attacks was that conven-
tional wisdom throughout the 1930s had suggested that simultaneous
attacks would lead to mutual destruction. In fact, both sides survived
attacks that should have destroyed them, and only one of the three carriers that were hit incurred, or seemed to have incurred, damage that
affected her battleworthiness. Both sides were determined to make
ready for a second strike in a battle that seemed to be just beginning.
However, the battle was over.

THREE REASONS together ensured that the Battle of the Coral Sea
ended with the single Japanese strike against TF 17. The first quickly
manifested itself, even as the two carrier forces set about recovering
aircraft in readiness for another strike: the Japanese were not in a position to renew offensive operations. Any attempt to continue the battle
would have involved just the *Zuikaku*, two heavy cruisers, and four
destroyers. The weakness of such a force was obvious, but no less a
weakness was that less than one-half of the aircraft with which the
Japanese had entered the Coral Sea remained. On 7 May the *Shokaku*
and *Zuikaku* between them mustered 121 aircraft, of which 109 were
operational. At one stage during the afternoon of 8 May the *Zuikaku*
had just nine operational aircraft. During the evening of 8 May this
total had risen to twenty-four Zekes, nine Vals, and six Kates, and by
the following morning twenty-four Zekes, thirteen Vals, and eight
Kates were available for operations. Thus, on the basis of an air group
with forty-five aircraft, the *Zuikaku* simply could not hope to do battle,
either offensively or defensively, over the Port Moresby area.

The second reason was one that was so basic as to be barely cred-
ible, but the fact was that neither during the run to the south from Truk

nor after it entered the Solomon Sea did the Japanese carrier force re-fuel. The result was that after the action on the morning of 8 May the escorts were so short of fuel that they could not contemplate even one high-speed action. Not one of the warships with the *Zuikaku* had tanks that were more than two-fifths full, and some were as low as one-fifth. After the *Zuikaku* had recovered aircraft, she and her escorts had no choice but to head north for a rendezvous with an oiler.

Such a situation was disastrous for the Japanese and ensured that Operation MO could not proceed. This point was recognized by Inoue, who nonetheless saw this reversal as only temporary and who, with Takagi and Vice Admiral Hara Chuichi, saw the battle in the Coral Sea as a victory. By their estimation, both enemy carriers had been sunk or very heavily damaged: the Americans were deemed incapable of further resistance. In these circumstances, abandoning Operation MO at this point was entirely sensible, especially if Nauru and Ocean were now picked up en passant. In the event, Inoue, who had been warned that the lateness of the strike on the morning of 8 May was likely to mean no second strike that day and possibly no strike the following morning, in orders issued at 1500 and confirmed with elaboration at 2300, recalled the various formations in the Solomon Sea, sent Takagi back to Truk, and postponed the assault on Port Moresby until 3 July. These orders should have ensured the end of the battle but were set aside by Yamamoto. At midnight the Combined Fleet directed all Japanese units to resume offensive operations and bring about the destruction of the enemy. Thirty-six hours were to pass, with Japanese warships vainly trying to find a trail that was more than twelve hours cold even when Yamamoto issued his instruction, before these ill-judged orders were rescinded. Operation MO was thereby assigned to the place that it should have occupied—after Operation MI—all along.

The third reason why the battle was not resumed related to the Americans. Thus far, they had been fortunate in that they had sunk the *Shoho* while escaping the consequences of their own success, and they appeared to have escaped remarkably lightly from their exchange with the *Shokaku* and *Zuikaku*. Both the *Lexington* and *Yorktown* had been hit, but the one more seriously damaged, the *Lexington*, had slowly built up her speed until she was making 25 knots at 1223. She was back on an even keel when around 1230 she turned into the wind to recover aircraft. Her elevators were still jammed and any aircraft that were recovered thus stood in danger of being jettisoned, but the crucial point was that the state of neither of the American ships was cause for anxiety.

Exactly what was happening within the ship is not known with certainty, but it is generally believed that fuel vapor escaping from ruptured tanks seeped into those parts of the *Lexington* that had been evacuated because of the breakdown of ventilation. Without a means of dispersal, the vapor became increasingly concentrated until at 1247 a spark from a generator that had been left running set off a huge explosion that destroyed the bulkhead between the generator and internal communications rooms, wrecked much of the telephone system, and, critically, killed or severely wounded many of the damage control personnel. It also destroyed the water main in this part of the ship. The *Lexington* continued to recover aircraft until 1414, but below deck a series of explosions progressively ravaged her. Without water to fight fires, the latter spread, igniting more vapor until a second massive explosion at 1445 wrecked the ventilation system of the boiler and engine rooms. Loss of power could not be prevented, and at 1456 the *Lexington* requested her escorts to stand by to take off survivors. After the engine room was shut down at 1630, the order to abandon ship was given at 1707. With a calm and warm sea and the carrier on an even keel and not under way, her cruisers and destroyers were able to pick up the hundreds of men left in the water. Indeed, it is believed that every man that entered the water alive was rescued. The *Lexington* sank at 1952 after the destroyer *Phelps* had administered the coup de grâce with five torpedoes.

Until the second explosion it was not clear that the *Lexington* was doomed. As the American carriers headed south away from the scene of the morning's exchanges, their attention focused largely on the possibility of mounting a second attack on the enemy carriers. The *Lexington*'s problem of recovering aircraft complicated matters, but the second explosion brought home the fact that a second attack, already highly unlikely because of the lateness of the hour, was problematical given the inability of the *Lexington* to transfer aircraft to the *Yorktown*. Although the *Yorktown* did recover nineteen of the *Lexington*'s aircraft, with thirty-six trapped on the *Lexington* the possibility of a second strike all but disappeared. But what ultimately told against any attempt to resume the battle was the simple fact that as the plight of the *Lexington* worsened, so it became correspondingly more important to ensure the safety of the *Yorktown*. Nimitz's order on the evening of 8 May to withdraw the *Yorktown* from the Coral Sea was undoubtedly sound, not least because of what was being discovered about Operation MI at this time. And here was the crux of the matter. With less than a month before Operations AL and MI, the *Yorktown* represented the difference between two and three carriers in the central Pacific. But, and no less important, with less than three weeks before units sailed for Operations AL and MI, there was no time for either side to consider carefully the events in the Coral Sea even though for both sides, and particularly for the Japanese, there were issues that, had time and temper allowed, would have been reason enough for pause and reconsideration of at least some of the assumptions that were the basis of action. As it was, such time was not available, given the immediacy of next-phase operations.

4

THE BATTLE OF MIDWAY

4–6 June 1942

With the various formations bound for the Aleutians and Midway sailing from their respective ports and anchorages between 27 and 29 May, the Japanese plan of campaign called for the Second Carrier Striking Force to conduct a series of strikes on Dutch Harbor on 3 June before the First Carrier Striking Force opened proceedings in the central Pacific with an attack on Midway soon after dawn on 4 June. Both formations planned on the basis of one single strike being insufficient to neutralize their respective targets.

Such intention incorporated three weaknesses. The most obvious was the assumption that events would unfold as anticipated and in a manner that would allow the Japanese to fight the battle exactly as planned. (Prussian Field Marshal Helmuth von Moltke's dictum, that no plan ever survives the first contact of battle, evidently had never been translated into Japanese.) The second was the desperately narrow margins on which the Japanese chose to operate. The two carriers allocated to the Aleutians deployed only thirty-three bombers between them, and for the dawn strike on Midway there were only 108 aircraft: the aircraft assigned to the second strike numbered just ninety-six. But with the four carriers of this formation assigned eighteen Zekes each, the total reserve held outside these allocations was three fighters with each carrier and nine Kates held with the *Kaga*. Such arrangements were, by the least exacting standard, marginal to requirements.

The third weakness concerned timings and details of the first strike and reconnaissance provision. The plan of the First Carrier Striking Force was that its mission against Midway should be flown off at the same time as reconnaissance and antisubmarine patrols were mounted. The latter patrol was to be conducted by two seaplanes from cruisers, while the reconnaissance effort was to involve the *Akagi* and *Kaga* both contributing their only scout plane, two seaplanes each from the *Chikuma* and *Tone*, and one seaplane from the *Haruna*. With only seven scouts directed to the disengaged flank, the search sectors did not overlap and there could be no two-phase reconnaissance with pre-dawn and post-dawn searches. With no reconnaissance conducted in advance of the launch of the strike against Midway, the Japanese plan all but invited problems.

Moreover, things began to go wrong for the Japanese even before the main formations sailed. Prior to the attack on Midway they planned to conduct a reconnaissance of Pearl Harbor with flying boats staged through French Frigate Shoals (Operation K). The submarine *I-121*, which was to refuel these flying boats, reached the Shoals on 26 May and subsequently was joined by the *I-123* with the *I-122* going on to Laysan. At the Shoals the *I-121* found one American seaplane tender and obvious signs of activity involving seaplanes and flying boats. On the 29th the Americans had a second unit in the Shoals, and the Japanese high command was informed accordingly. Operation K was therefore postponed for a day, but with the next day bringing no change in the situation, the operation was abandoned.

Nagumo's carrier force, as it advanced toward Midway, was not informed that Operation K had been abandoned, nor was it informed that by 30 May the scale of radio traffic off Pearl Harbor suggested that an American carrier task group was off the Hawaiian Islands and that there appeared to be a gathering of American submarines to the west of Midway. Moreover, it was not advised that on 31 May and 1 June there were clashes between Japanese flying boats from Wake and their American opposite numbers from Midway. Nagumo's formation was also not privy to the information, passed by the submarine *I-168*, which had spent three days watching the atoll from periscope depth, of activity on Midway that included some ninety to one hundred reconnaissance missions per day and round-the-clock construction of facilities. Perhaps no single item of activity amounted to much, but together they suggested a pattern of enemy behavior that should have inspired the utmost caution. But Nagumo's force was never informed of any of these developments any more than it was advised that the submarine scouting lines that were supposed to be in place astride the Hawaiian Islands were not completed on time. As it was, Task Force 16 would have escaped detection even if the Japanese submarines had arrived on station on time, but Task Force 17, with the *Yorktown*, passed through the B search line just before midnight on 31 May, a matter of hours ahead of late-arriving Japanese submarines.

For all their efforts, however, the Americans failed to find the Japanese carrier force during the approach-to-contact phase. The American command on Midway hoped to secure early sighting of enemy formations as they neared Midway that would enable land-based bombers to attack while the atoll itself remained beyond the range of Japanese aircraft. On 3 June it pushed out reconnaissance missions to a distance of 700 miles west of Midway, but the day passed with the Americans able to mount only two attacks on Japanese formations. One attack, by nine B-17 Flying Fortresses, was directed against the transport force, but not one Japanese ship was damaged. The other attack was staged overnight by four Catalinas, one of which managed to torpedo the *Akebono Maru*, although the tanker kept her place in formation.

On 3 June the main events were in the Aleutians, and the fact that operations here unfolded in accordance with Japanese intentions was a source of reassurance for both sides. Here the Japanese carriers committed aircraft against Dutch Harbor shortly after dawn. The *Junyo* provided Vals and Zekes, the *Ryujo* Kates and Zekes, but the formations became separated and the twelve Vals, with their escorting Zekes, were obliged to return to their carrier. The aircraft from the *Ryujo*, on the other hand, flew into the first clear weather over Dutch Harbor in three days and successfully struck at oil dumps, the hospital, and barracks. One Zeke was lost shooting down a Catalina, but as the Japanese aircraft withdrew they chanced upon the destroyers in Makushin Bay. Thus alerted to the enemy's presence, they attempted a second attack, which was primarily entrusted to the Vals from the *Junyo*. These planes, however, failed to find their targets for a second time, and only four seaplanes were able to mount attacks. All four were lost, two to P-40 fighters and two during recovery, while the Americans lost four Catalinas to weather and two to Zekes. With the balance of incapability imposing itself evenly, by late afternoon the Second Carrier Striking Force retired to ready itself for a renewed effort the following day. Events off Midway the next morning, however, meant that the intention to continue offensive operations in the Aleutians was immediately suspended.

DURING THE NIGHT OF 3–4 JUNE, as the Second Carrier Striking Force marked time in the north, the First Carrier Striking Force increased speed to be in its flying-off position with the dawn. At the same time the Americans on Midway were preparing their air formations for reconnaissance, combat air patrol, and strike missions. At 0415 on 4 June eleven Catalina amphibians were despatched while sixteen B-17 Flying Fortresses were committed against the transport force to the west. Six Wildcats were held as the dawn combat air patrol, and at sea the carriers committed ten Dauntless scouts to the same role. Within fifteen more minutes the Japanese carriers had begun to launch the aircraft committed to the initial strike against Midway, and within another fifteen minutes these aircraft, in their attack formation, had set off for the atoll at a speed of 125 knots. They left behind a formation making 25 knots as it sought to cut down the distance that returning aircraft would have to fly after having attacked Midway. Little note was taken of the fact that both of the cruisers experienced difficulty in despatching seaplanes on scouting duties. The *Chikuma*'s second seaplane developed engine problems on its catapult; and although it was launched a little later than scheduled, it was quickly forced to return.

The *Tone*'s catapult launching mechanism jammed with the result that her second seaplane was not flown off until 0500. The second of the *Tone*'s seaplanes was reported by a Catalina from Midway at 0534. Some six minutes later a second Catalina, encountering Japanese aircraft, sent a signal to Midway that gave advance warning of the impending raid. It was not until 0552 that the Japanese carrier force was sighted, two carriers being reported. With intelligence pointing to the Japanese having four or five carriers, a report that cited two presented Fletcher with obvious difficulties. Having decided to proceed with an attack, at 0607 Fletcher divided his forces. While the *Yorktown* recovered aircraft from the combat air patrol, the *Enterprise* and *Hornet* settled on a course that ensured convergence with Japanese carriers assumed to be closing on Midway. With the *Yorktown* following the *Enterprise* and *Hornet*, the U.S. carriers would be able to launch their aircraft about 0700 and the latter would contact the Japanese carriers, at a range of about 155 miles from the American formations, at or about 0830.

Radar at Midway picked up the incoming Japanese force at a range of ninety-three miles, and by an unfortunate sequence of events the greater part of American bombers on Midway were on the ground as the Japanese approached. The last bomber left Midway with Japanese aircraft less than thirty miles distant, but they set out without fighter escort. Nonetheless, and to use a Japanese observation at the time, the fact that the bombers did get away meant that Midway was like a snake that had crawled away leaving its cast-off skin to be attacked. The Japanese shattered the fighter force held in defense. The hangars and oil dumps on Sand Island and the power station on Eastern Island were destroyed, but clearly the attack failed to neutralize the atoll, and at 0700 the flight commander signaled Nagumo and the carriers his view that a second, follow-up strike would be necessary.

This signal was received at a time when the Japanese carrier force came under attack by bombers from Midway. The first to arrive were six Avengers and four Marauders, which dived in succession with the result that both sets of aircraft were cut to pieces. One Avenger and two Marauders survived the combat air patrol, and two of these were heavily damaged: the only aircraft that came within effective range was a heavily damaged Marauder that tried to crash itself into the *Akagi*. About 0715, as this attack ended, Nagumo predictably ordered that the

Kates held in readiness with a torpedo armament be taken below and rearmed for a second attack on Midway.

Nagumo's decision went to the heart of the Japanese dilemma in this operation. The rearming of the Kates, refueling of Zekes, and readying of formations would take about ninety minutes with another thirty minutes needed to fly off the second strike, and the aircraft returning from Midway could be expected to arrive over the carriers between 0815 and 0830. The various timings indicated that the Japanese might well face an option of difficulties, but as long as there was only one target, Midway, it was likely that whatever difficulties arose could be negotiated. At 0728, however, Nagumo's force received a sighting report of an American task group made by the seaplane from the *Tone* that had been delayed. How the American formation escaped detection by one of the Jakes from the *Chikuma* is one of the puzzles of Midway, as is the perverse fact that the seaplane that found the formation failed to note the presence of carriers.

This signal caused some fifteen minutes of deliberations on the *Akagi* and ended with the decision to halt the rearming of the Kates and the sending of a signal to the *Tone*'s seaplane asking for clarification. What seems extraordinary is that no one on the carrier staff asked the obvious question of why the Americans should be where they were, and on their reported course, unless they had carriers. But if the staff of the carrier force failed in this respect, then the attitude aboard the fleet flagship, the *Yamato*, appears incredible. There was no concern that the basic premise of the Midway plan— that the Americans could only react to events—was clearly dead and buried. The enemy's unanticipated appearance merely meant the destruction of American forces so much the sooner, and the greater the victory in the process. There seems to have been absolutely no appreciation that Nagumo, at that moment, faced a three-day schedule reduced to thirty minutes.

Nagumo's problems were compounded by the fact that at the very time when the counterorder about arming and the request-for-clarification signal were made, there began a series of attacks by aircraft from Midway that was to last until 0830. The first formation to arrive was a force of sixteen Dauntlesses. Between 0755 and 0812 this force attacked the *Hiryu* and *Soryu*, the former escaping with five near-misses; in return, half the Dauntlesses were destroyed. As this attack came to

an end, at 0809, Nagumo's carrier force learned that the enemy formation consisted of five cruisers and five destroyers, but it had no time to
dwell on the significance of the message before a high-level B-17 Flying Fortress attack, from 20,000 feet, began. Between 0814 and about
0819 nine Flying Fortresses straddled but failed to hit the *Hiryu* and
Soryu, and as this attack ended so the last of the bombers from Midway, eleven aging Vindicators, arrived. Attacking from mid-altitude
and seeking out the nearest target, the battleship *Haruna*, two of the
Vindicators were shot down and another four were badly damaged
by Zekes. This attack, which like all the others failed to register a single
hit, took place between 0817 and 0830. It had just started when the
carrier force received a signal from the *Tone*'s seaplane reporting the
presence of what seemed to be an aircraft carrier with the American
task force.

THIS SIGNAL INITIATED what has generally been portrayed by most
historians as the critical phase of the battle for the Japanese. The report,
along with a second signal sent at 0830 that noted the presence of two
additional cruisers, set in motion a sequence of events that ended disastrously, and the general line of criticism directed against Nagumo is
that he should have ordered an immediate attack without waiting to
recover aircraft returning from their mission against Midway.

Objective analysis of the situation at this stage suggests three conclusions. First, the First Carrier Striking Force had very little option but
to forgo an immediate second strike. The force that it could put into
the air at this time would have had few fighters to escort the bombers,
and the past hour had provided ample evidence of what happened to
strike aircraft not afforded proper fighter escort. The problem was that
Zekes from the combat air patrol would have to be landed and made
ready, but with the return of aircraft from Midway the Japanese problem of timings was obvious. Nagumo had no real choice but to recover
these aircraft because if he chose to recover the Zekes and then launch
a strike, then perhaps as many as one-third, and possibly two-fifths, of
the survivors from the attack on Midway could easily be lost. The Japanese carriers could no more afford such losses than they could afford

those likely to be incurred by bombers committed to an attack without adequate escort.

The second conclusion would note one of the most important criticisms made of these decisions, that given by Commander Fuchida Mitsuo in *Midway: The Battle that Doomed Japan*:

> . . . there was no question that it would have been wiser to launch our dive-bombers immediately, even without fighter protection. In such all-or-nothing carrier warfare, no other choice was admissible. Even the risk of sending unprotected level-bombers should have been accepted as necessary in this emergency. Their fate would probably have been the same as that of the unescorted American planes which had attacked us a short while before, but just possibly they might have saved us from the catastrophe we were about to suffer.[1]

First published in 1955, this statement inadvertently proved that Fuchida, in thirteen years, never understood the problem of which he was so critical. No attack by Japanese forces at this stage "might have saved us from the catastrophe we were about to suffer" because the American aircraft that were to strike down three Japanese carriers had already left their flight decks. There was no way in which a strike against the Japanese carriers could have undone that fact, which, taking place after 0702, was key to the events of the battle. At best, a Japanese attack might have resulted in an equalization of losses, but an attack could never have prevented the catastrophe that engulfed the Japanese.

The third and last conclusion is that in very large part the First Carrier Striking Force was able to get itself into a position where it was ready to strike with its full available strength when it was overwhelmed. Any careful evaluation of the Japanese situation will consider that by 0900 the carrier force had more or less recovered its balance. The real point of criticism should be directed not so much against the decisions made or not made by Nagumo, with one possible exception, but rather to a plan of campaign that left the First Carrier Striking Force exposed to defeat in detail and a failure on the part of Yamamoto and the Combined Fleet staff to keep the carrier formation fully informed of developments that directly affected its operations and safety.

The one possible exception—the decision by Nagumo—that does invite criticism was the one that committed the Japanese carriers, once they had recovered their aircraft from the Midway strike, to steer a course that reduced the distance between themselves and the American

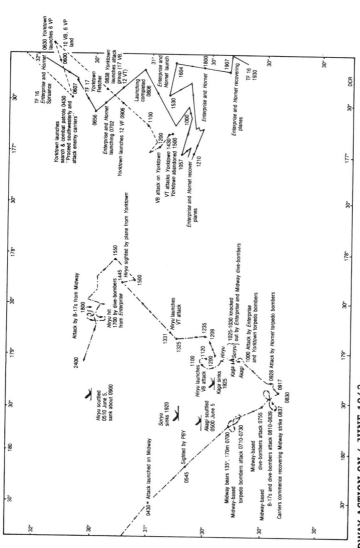

BATTLE OF MIDWAY ACTION ON 4 JUNE 1942

From H. P. Willmott, *The Barrier and the Javelin: Japanese and Allied Pacific Strategies, February to June 1942* (Annapolis: Naval Institute Press, 1983), 366.

carriers. The first of the Midway aircraft, plus fighters from the combat air patrol, were recovered by 0900, the last at 0917. Within another minute the Japanese carriers had begun to turn onto a course, with a bearing of 70 degrees, that was designed to close the distance between themselves and the enemy. Such was the haste of the Japanese formation that it did not reverse order, with the result that the carriers steamed in a roughly rhombic pattern with the *Hiryu* leading, the *Soryu* and *Akagi* roughly abreast of one another, and the *Kaga* astern of the *Soryu*. With the ships of the screen seemingly cast randomly around, the turn after 0918 seems to have no logic or reason. The point, however, is that at this stage the carrier force needed to buy time and ready itself for a strike against the American formation. It had scouts both in contact and on their way to the enemy formation to ensure that contact was not lost. But Nagumo did not take his force away from the enemy aircraft that he knew after 0855 were heading for his ships. Steering to the west in the hope that the enemy strike would hit the empty sea or to the north may not have evaded every enemy squadron, but either course might have bought the Japanese carriers those extra minutes that they needed.

Inevitably, because the Japanese lost this battle, the attention of History has concentrated on their plan of campaign and conduct of operations, and the basic line that has been followed over the years has been that they largely brought defeat upon themselves. Such a conclusion cannot be denied, but it could be said that the American conduct of operations came close to snatching defeat from the jaws of victory. Two aspects of this conduct of operations—the twin facts that between 0552 and 0838 Fletcher received no signal reporting the strength, position, and course of the First Carrier Striking Force and that Task Force 16 took an hour to launch a total of 117 aircraft while the *Yorktown* did not begin to launch her aircraft until 0838, or thirty-two minutes after the *Enterprise* and *Hornet* had completed flying off their aircraft—provide ample evidence of such a charge. With the *Enterprise* and *Hornet* being delayed in the launching of their Devastators and Wildcats, the two carriers had to send out their Dauntless bombers without fighter cover because after forty minutes in the air they could not be held any longer. What should have been perhaps two set-piece attacks thus ended in six separate and uncoordinated attacks. This fragmentation of effort, this lack of concentration and coordination, should have ensured failure but perversely produced success.

THE FIRST ATTACKS on the Japanese force by the U.S. carrier squadrons certainly were less than impressive. In committing their squadrons to the offensive, the operations staff provided a course of 239 degrees based on the assumption that the Japanese carriers would continue to close on Midway after launching their aircraft, but the Japanese formation was to the north of where the American staff had calculated it to be because it had lost time in beating off the attacks made by aircraft from Midway. Moreover, it had then turned onto a course that would have taken it astern of the American formations and hence north and clear of American aircraft seeking contact on the prescribed 239-degree course. If all these aircraft had flown this course, none would have sighted the enemy carriers, and such was the fate of the Dauntlesses and Wildcats from the *Hornet*. These planes flew the set course until 0930, by which time they should have been directly over the enemy formation. With visibility good in all directions, the aircraft encountered empty ocean. The air group commander chose to believe that the enemy was likely between him and Midway, and therefore the American aircraft began to search to the south. As fuel needles began to near the empty mark, Kure was seen and then the fires on Midway. Without sufficient fuel to search to the north, the attack had to be abandoned. With little or no chance of being able to get back to the *Hornet*, most of the Dauntlesses tried to land at Midway. Three were forced to ditch (two in the lagoon), but amazingly one of the Dauntless bombers made it back to the *Hornet*, although five of the Dauntless scouts that attempted to do the same were lost. All of the fighters, which attempted to regain the *Hornet* rather than try to land on Midway, went down. Thus, the largest of the individual formations sent against the Japanese carriers failed to secure a contact with the enemy and lost two-fifths of its strength in the process. Ten Wildcats and eight Dauntlesses had been lost, and another eleven Dauntlesses were out of the battle for the moment.

The *Hornet*'s remaining squadron did find the enemy, mainly because it had expected to do so north of the calculated position. The torpedo-bombers met the enemy as the latter turned away from Midway, just after 0918, but under conditions that were disastrous. The Devastators should have been afforded fighter cover, but during the

Wildcats' climb to medium altitude visual contact had been lost and the *Hornet*'s fighters aligned themselves with Devastators from the *Enterprise*. Thus, in pressing their attack, the *Hornet*'s fifteen torpedo-bombers were wholly unsupported. The attack rightly entered U.S. naval lore because in accordance with the expressed wishes of the squadron commander, Lieutenant Commander John C. Waldron, that all aircraft should press home the attack without regard to the consequences, the Devastators, formed into an extended line for search-and-attack purposes, were met by a combat air patrol that accounted for every American aircraft. Only one pilot survived an attack that the Japanese carriers evaded with ease.

The trails left by Japanese fighters moving against the *Hornet*'s torpedo-bombers drew the attention of the Devastators from the *Enterprise*. They had flown the prescribed 239-degree course and found nothing, and like the *Hornet*'s formation searched to the north when signs of battle attracted their notice at a range of thirty miles. At 0930, by which time the *Hornet*'s torpedo-bombers had been destroyed, the enemy carriers were sighted. In seeking to attack, the Devastators, coming from the south, had to work their way from astern around the flank of a fast-moving enemy to positions from which to mount their assault. The Devastators split themselves into two forces in the hope of dividing the Zekes and Japanese antiaircraft fire, but the combat air patrol accounted for ten of the Devastators before the survivors simply aimed themselves at the nearest carrier, the *Kaga*, and launched their torpedoes as best they could. Such improvization ensured the escape of these four Dauntlesses. The *Kaga* evaded the torpedoes aimed at her with ease.

This attack took place between 0940 and about 1005, and scarcely had it ended than a third attack, by the Devastators from the *Yorktown*, began. Unlike the torpedo-bombers from the other two carriers, the twelve from the *Yorktown* had fighter support in the shape of six Wildcats, but the Japanese combat air patrol at this stage was in strength and at low level, and hence able to move immediately against the American formation. Moreover, the incoming American aircraft were sighted by Japanese cruisers at a range of eighteen miles. This combination of Japanese advantages served to ensure that ten of the Devastators were destroyed, seven before they had a chance to launch their torpedoes. The Japanese carriers avoided this last torpedo attack with the same ease as they had avoided the attacks by the Devastators from the *Enterprise* and *Hornet*.

This final Devastator attack on the Japanese carrier force began at about 1000 and ended about 1020, and it was the last of the attacks that failed to result in damage to any Japanese warship. But between them the three Devastator sorties achieved two things. The Japanese, knowing that these aircraft had not come from Midway, were suddenly made aware that at least two American carriers were at sea, and the Zekes of the Japanese combat air patrol were concentrated at low altitude at the very time when the Dauntlesses from the *Enterprise* and *Yorktown* arrived over the Japanese carriers. With no aircraft at high altitude, the American bombers encountered no resistance as they moved to attack the Japanese carriers. The latter had nearly completed the rearming and refueling of all the serviceable aircraft that had returned from the attack on Midway. These planes were being serviced within the carriers' hangars while the flight decks were reserved for aircraft from the combat air patrol. The Japanese carriers were perhaps thirty to forty minutes from being able to move, spot, and launch the aircraft for the second strike. Moreover, what they had not been able to buy themselves was the 7.5 minutes that the Zekes needed to climb to 20,000 feet. The chance that the American staffs had identified at the 27 May conference was about to present itself. The Japanese carriers had escaped being caught in the process of recovering, rearming, and refueling their aircraft, but time had not allowed for the proper stowing of spare ammunition, draining of fuel lines, and removal of bowsers from the flight and hangar decks.

MORE THAN TWO DECADES were to pass after the end of the Second World War before passions cooled, claims and counterclaims were adjusted, and the events that followed the arrival of the Dauntlesses over the First Carrier Striking Force were subjected to some form of authoritative and impartial examination by Walter Long in *Incredible Victory*. It was Long who noted with irony the basic problems of trying to determine what happened in this next phase of the battle: "If the squadron action reports are taken at face value, everybody hit the *Akagi*

or the *Kaga*. Nobody claims the *Soryu*—she presumably got back to Japan. But if the specific recollections of the three attack leaders are accepted, nobody got the *Akagi*. Each is convinced his target had its island [top of superstructure] on the starboard side—yet the *Akagi*'s island was to port."[2] Moreover, there was considerable resentment on the part of the *Yorktown*'s pilots in being afforded the credit for sinking the *Soryu* and not either of the much larger *Akagi* and *Kaga*.

Most of the discrepancies of the available record can be reconciled on the basis of four assumptions: 1) that the Dauntlesses from the *Enterprise* approached the Japanese formation from the southwest whereas the Dauntlesses from the *Yorktown* approached the enemy from off the enemy's starboard bow; 2) that the various attacking squadrons fortuitously attacked different targets and did not cross one another's paths in their approaches; 3) that the Japanese carriers were in a rough line-ahead formation; and 4) that the *Soryu* and the *Akagi* had exchanged positions with the *Soryu* ahead and slightly to starboard of the *Akagi*. The last two assumptions were the really contentious ones, but it appears that to avoid the *Yorktown*'s Devastators the *Akagi* had presented her stern as she turned to port and passed astern of the *Soryu*, the two units thereby changing position. For her part the *Kaga* seems to have turned to starboard to avoid both the Devastators' torpedoes and the *Akagi*, and that thereafter she had both the *Soryu* and *Akagi* slightly to port.

This phase of the battle unfolded with the Dauntlesses from the *Enterprise*, having gone to the south of the Japanese position, locating the enemy carrier formation courtesy of the lone Japanese destroyer *Arashi*. She had been left behind after the American submarine *Nautilus*, finding herself in the company of the First Carrier Striking Force, had fired two torpedoes at a Japanese battleship: as the carriers hurried on, the *Arashi* had been left to keep down or destroy the *Nautilus*. Sighted when she was steaming to rejoin her parent formation, the *Arashi* inadvertently pointed the way for the *Enterprise*'s Dauntlesses. When the latter encountered the Japanese formation, the Dauntlesses divided by squadron, with the bombers moving against the *Kaga* and the scouts against the *Akagi*.

The *Kaga*, the first of the three carriers to be attacked and hit, was struck by the fourth bomb aimed at her and then by three of the next five. The first hit landed among the Kates waiting to take off. The second and third hits were in the area of the second elevator, near the bridge, and the fourth hit was registered in the center of the flight deck. These hits set off a series of detonations within the ship. So quickly was the *Kaga* engulfed that the last of the bombers that were to attack her switched their attention to the *Akagi*, so obviously and rapidly was the *Kaga* doomed.

The *Akagi*, the second carrier to be hit, was struck by only two bombs. The first hit her on the edge of her center elevator, penetrated the shaft, and set off torpedoes and bombs that had not been returned to the magazines. These explosions would have been enough to doom the ship even without the second hit, in the port quarter, among the aircraft, ordnance, and fuel lines on the deck. The force of the explosions thus induced carried through the *Akagi*, jamming the rudder 20 degrees of port, and sweeping the entire flight deck with a wall of flame. Only the prompt flooding of the forward magazine kept the ship from blowing herself to pieces.

The *Soryu*, the last of the three Japanese carriers to be bombed, was attacked by Dauntlesses from the *Yorktown* that left three hits well spaced along her flight deck. Her forward and central elevators were destroyed, the former being cast from its housing against the island. A series of massive explosions were set off, and within a matter of minutes the *Soryu* had lost steering and power. As early as 1045 the order to abandon ship was given.

What remained of 4 June was spent by most of the screening units of the First Carrier Striking Force trying to save the stricken carriers and evacuate personnel, but all three carriers were doomed from the time that they were hit. They were doomed for two common reasons, of which one was obvious: all three were littered with ordnance that had not been returned to the magazines and had flight decks with open fuel lines and bowsers because it had not been possible to lower Zekes to the hangar decks for rearming and refueling. With crews working on the hangar deck on aircraft that had returned from Midway and on the flight deck with Zekes from the combat air patrol, and at the same time beginning to spot aircraft for the strike against the American formation that had been found, the Japanese carriers were peculiarly vulnerable at the time they were hit.

The second reason was more fundamental. Of all navies, the Kaigun was the least concerned with defensive requirements for its carriers. The *Soryu* had just 1 inch of armor over her machinery and 2 inches over her magazines and aviation fuel. The *Hiryu* had

3.5 inches of armor over her tanks but was only partially compartmentalized. The *Akagi* and *Kaga*, having been laid down originally as capital ships, had casements and belts but were no better protected horizontally than the *Hiryu* and *Soryu*. Japanese carriers were built around speed and ease of handling, not least in terms of having three elevators in flight decks that provided their longitudinal strength. Hangar decks were not flash- and vapor-tight. The basic fact about Japanese carriers was that they were poorly built; indeed, some of the Kaigun's wartime conversions were among the most badly built ships in any navy. Moreover, with numbers of crewmen not much more than one-half of those in the American service, Japanese carriers were undermanned in such critical matters as damage control. In the *Kaga*'s case, however, this was not a major factor in her loss because the bombs that hit her wiped out her damage control parties and wrecked the pumps and other equipment needed to bring her fires under control.

From the outset the position of the *Kaga* was hopeless. The first two bombs that hit her utterly devastated the flight and hangar decks, while the third bomb exploded near the bridge, killing or wounding everyone there and igniting a gasoline wagon that exploded over the island, killing everyone in the ship's control centers. With uncontrollable fires gradually spreading throughout, with power faltering, and with the *Kaga* acquiring a list, the first stage in the process of abandoning ship took place at 1325 when the Emperor's portrait was transferred to the destroyer *Hagikaze*. The order to abandon ship was finally given at 1700, and not before the *Kaga* survived an attack by the *Nautilus*. Drawn to the scene by the carriers' fires, she worked her way through the screens to fire four torpedoes at an almost stationary *Kaga*. One torpedo refused to leave its tube, two ran deep, and the one that hit the carrier failed to explode and broke in two. With the warhead sinking, the lighter rear section of the torpedo became a life-saver for members of the *Kaga*'s crew already in the water. The *Kaga* began to settle at about 1900, and when fires reached her forward aviation fuel tanks she was all but blown apart. She rolled over and sank at 1925. The *Soryu* likewise suffered progressive destruction as fires raged through her, and she settled by the stern at 1912. Within three minutes she had sunk, a massive underwater explosion occurring at 1920. She, like the *Kaga*, lost about seven hundred of her crew.

The *Akagi* demonstrated a more tenacious hold on life, although from the time that she was hit it was recognized that she could no longer function as the flagship. Nagumo and his staff were transferred first to the destroyer *Nowaki* at 1046 and then to the light cruiser *Nagara* at 1130. Even by the time that Nagumo left the ship, she had lost steering and all communications and was losing power. With smoke suffocating the men in the engine rooms, the boilers were shut down at 1042, and thereafter the fight to contain and extinguish her fires was a slowly failing one. The first order to remove members of the crew not involved in firefighting was given at 1130. At 1350, some ten minutes after the transfer of the Emperor's portrait, the *Akagi* lost power and began to drift, and after 1400 there began her systematic evacuation, which lasted until 2000. Her captain refused to abandon his ship and was left tied to the anchor deck. At 0300 on the following morning, with the *Akagi* refusing to sink, she was boarded and the captain forcibly removed. She was sunk by torpedoes from the *Nowaki* just after dawn.

EVEN BEFORE NAGUMO LEFT the *Akagi*, the *Hiryu* turned into the wind to launch eighteen Vals and six Zekes. The commander of the Second Carrier Division, Rear Admiral Yamaguchi Tamon, had urged Nagumo to fly off a strike at 0830, before the aircraft returning from Midway had been recovered. Having had his worst fears realized, Yamaguchi was determined to strike immediately now that the balance of vulnerabilities had been reversed: having conducted an attack that had accounted for three enemy carriers, the American carriers now had the task of recovering, refueling, and rearming their returning aircraft while the enemy had no such obligations. The Japanese problem, however, was that the balance of vulnerabilities had not been reversed to the extent that gave the *Hiryu* any realistic chances of overturning the imbalance of losses. At this stage, Yamaguchi did not know that his command faced three American carriers, and it was the third, separate from the other two, that made a difficult task next to impossible, although with the *Hornet* having lost virtually all her offensive capability either at sea or to Midway, more unnecessary American loss was experienced. With the *Enterprise* well short of where she was supposed to meet her returning aircraft, eighteen Dauntlesses were obliged to ditch short of their carrier, and only two managed to reach the

Yorktown. The result was that after the morning strike, Task Force 16 retained only a minor offensive capability.

The *Yorktown*'s aircraft were able to find the carrier with little difficulty; the only problem was that they led Japanese aircraft to her. Unknown to the Japanese, however, American radar had IFF (identification, friend or foe) capability and the incoming Japanese were found at a range of sixty-five miles. The *Yorktown*, which had recovered Dauntlesses from TF 16 and her own Wildcats, immediately set about draining fuel lines, consigning a fuel bowser on the flight deck to the deep, and after 1150 despatching ten Dauntlesses in pairs on reconnaissance to a distance of 250 miles in an attempt to ensure that contact with the enemy was retained. Waving off her own dive-bombers, fifteen of which were recovered by the *Enterprise*, the *Yorktown*, with two heavy cruisers and five destroyers, worked up to 30 knots even as Wildcats from the combat air patrol shot down six Vals in cruise formation. With another five Vals destroyed before the Japanese dive-bombers could attack, between 1205 and 1216 the *Yorktown* was assailed by only seven Vals. She was left dead in the water as a result of three hits and three near-misses.

The first of the bombs to hit the *Yorktown* was the one that did the most damage. It sliced its way to the level of the second deck and exploded at the base of the uptakes from the boiler room. The force of the explosion knocked out five of the six boilers in service, and by 1220 the *Yorktown* had lost power. Although she was not in any danger of sinking, she could not work her guns and could not operate aircraft, and with no communications she could no longer function as the flagship. Accordingly, between 1300 and 1311 Fletcher and his staff left her and at 1324 had established themselves on the heavy cruiser *Astoria*.

The second of the bombs to hit the *Yorktown* tumbled in flight with the result that it exploded on the flight deck. An area ten feet square was destroyed, with the force of the explosion taken by some of the starboard gun positions. Loss of life in these positions was heavy, but the ship was spared real damage from this bomb by the fact that although the blast reached into the hangar deck where seven Dauntlesses were being serviced, the spray system used in all American carriers checked the fires but three Dauntlesses were lost. The *Yorktown* was also spared real damage by the fact that the third bomb to hit her sliced through the flight and hangar decks via the forward elevator and landed in a rag store: a matter of feet either way and it would have exploded in either the 5-inch shell magazine or the forward avgas compartments. As it was, the fires from the second hit were seen from the *Enterprise* more than twenty miles away.

SUCCESS IN LEAVING the *Yorktown* stationary and burning fiercely appeared to provide the Japanese with a double opportunity. The Americans, recovering aircraft at the time of the attack, had to be a minimum of two hours away from readying their aircraft for a second strike. Now, with what seemed one-half of the American strength out of action, the *Hiryu* prepared for another attack, although with the loss of sixteen aircraft in the last one she had no reserve with which to press any advantage. Having recovered aircraft from the Midway strike, the *Hiryu* could muster only ten Kates, one of which was a stray from the *Akagi*, plus six Zekes, two of which hailed from the *Kaga*. In preparing for another strike the flight commander ordered his damaged Kate to be made ready, knowing that it could not be provided with fuel for a return trip. These aircraft were committed to the attack at 1331 with very clear instructions to ignore one stationary carrier.

Although the initiative for the moment lay with the *Hiryu*, the balance of advantage increasingly favored the Americans from this time. It did so in part because scouting by the *Yorktown* ensured that contact with the *Hiryu* was made and retained, and from this fact flowed a number of matters that combined to ensure her destruction. In effect, Fletcher's decision to despatch ten Dauntlesses proved a reconnaissance for TF 16, which after its morning's losses could not have mounted a reconnaissance on its own. The *Yorktown* also provided the *Enterprise* with the equivalent of the dive-bomber squadron, while in the second half of the afternoon eleven of the Dauntlesses that had landed on Midway made their way back to the *Hornet*. The overall result was that in addition to what the *Yorktown* retained, the *Enterprise* and *Hornet* together mustered about one carrier's worth of bombers while the *Hiryu*, after launching her third strike mission of the day, had virtually nothing left in reserve.

It was only after the *Hiryu* had committed her last aircraft to this attack that the Japanese realized, for the first time, that they faced three American carriers, not two. This information was elicited from a Judy reconnaissance aircraft from the *Soryu*, which, with a defective radio, returned to the *Hiryu* after the latter had launched her third strike mission. It was confirmed by a prisoner who had been plucked from the water by the *Arashi* and who was axed to death after interrogation. For the first time, therefore, the Japanese were made aware that even after having hammered one enemy carrier, they faced not one but two carriers: the chances of an understrength strike by Kates against one carrier were not good, but against two were barely existent. And some thirty minutes after the *Hiryu* began to launch her aircraft, and unseen by any Japanese eye after the reconnaissance seaplane from the *Chikuma* watching over Task Force 17 was shot down by a Wildcat from TF 16, the *Yorktown* began moving under her own power.

At 1340, more than an hour after the Japanese attack, four of the *Yorktown*'s boilers were brought back on line: by 1350 she had steam for 20 knots, and at 1402 she began moving under her own power. By 1417 she was making 17 knots but was not able to launch her aircraft, and her radar and plotting facilities remained out of action. At about 1428 the Kates and Zekes from the *Hiryu*'s third attack force came across her and her escorts, and not unnaturally the Japanese aircrew never considered that this was the carrier reportedly burning furiously and dead in the water. The Kates immediately moved into the attack, losing the first of their number to a six-strong combat air patrol provided by the *Enterprise*. The Kates divided into two five-strong sections to try to mount a scissors attack, but the *Yorktown*'s turn-away left one of these sections with an extended approach in which Wildcats and flak accounted for every aircraft.

Only four Kates were able to launch torpedoes at the carrier but two of them struck her in the region of Frames 75 and 90 on the port side and, ripping open the *Yorktown* over 65 feet of her length, caused massive destruction to the boiler and generator rooms. Because she was turning when hit, her rudder was jammed at 15 degrees to port, and she took on a 6-degree list to port immediately. With the inflow of water, which extinguished her fires, the *Yorktown* took on a 30-degree list before easing to 26 degrees at 1455, some fourteen minutes after she was hit. With the force of the explosion and water wrecking and warping many of the watertight doors to the third deck, the *Yorktown* was in danger of being lost to progressive flooding, and the order to abandon ship was given at 1458. Men went over the side as all the destroyers lowered boats and began the task of picking up survivors. Ultimately three of the destroyers picked up some 1,800 of the 2,200-man crew, at some risk to their own stability. At this time, however, the major events of the latter part of the day were being shaped by two sets of decisions: one taken on the *Enterprise*, and the other on the *Hiryu*.

Perhaps strangely, the decisions were the same: the carriers were to undertake one more offensive effort. The American decision was what could be expected: the survivors of the morning attack had been recovered and those fit to continue operations brought to readiness. The Japanese decision was not necessarily what might have been expected: the *Hiryu* had launched three strike missions and must have been close to exhaustion; more important, she had only six Kates and six Vals for an attack. But the *Hiryu* was committed to a fourth and last operation because it was believed that two enemy carriers had been seriously damaged. Originally, an attack was to be launched at 1630, but it was postponed in the hope that if launched around 1600, dusk would afford the bombers a degree of protection that would otherwise be denied them.

With Yamamoto and the whole of the Combined Fleet seemingly making for Midway at full speed, with the Aleutians venture halted to bring two carriers to the south more quickly, and with the *Hiryu* assumed to have knocked out two enemy carriers in the fight, there was perhaps something to be said for a third strike in an attempt to ensure an equalization of losses. Against that, however, was the simple fact that if the *Hosho, Junyo, Ryujo*, and *Zuiho* were to be committed to the battle, then it was vital for the *Hiryu* to survive, and that meant that she clear the battle area immediately: her survival was more important than any loss she might be able to inflict on the enemy. But once the *Hiryu* had flown off her aircraft at 1331 the initiative lay with the Americans, and with the range between forces coming down to about 110 miles during the afternoon and the Americans having reestablished contact with the *Hiryu* and her escorts at 1420, the *Hiryu* was far more vulnerable than her admiral and captain realized.

With the decision to launch a strike against the lone Japanese carrier still in the battle, the *Enterprise* turned into the wind at 1530 and launched twenty-five Dauntlesses, one of which was forced to return to the carrier almost immediately. Of the remaining aircraft, ten, from the *Enterprise,* were under orders to attack the *Hiryu*, and fourteen, from the *Yorktown*, were invited to earn their keep at the expense of members of her screen. The *Hornet* was supposed to have contributed to the attack, but orders to her were so mismanaged that she was unaware both of the *Hiryu*'s position and what was expected of her. But with the timely return of her sixteen Dauntlesses from Midway, the *Hornet* was able to hurriedly refuel these aircraft and began to launch them at 1603. They were, however, superfluous. The aircraft from the *Enterprise* first found the *Akagi*, *Kaga*, and *Soryu* and their escorts and then found the *Hiryu* and her screen some forty miles to the north. With the Dauntlesses sighted before they reached the point of attack, a combination of Zekes, flak, and high-speed maneuvering on the part of the carrier was enough to ensure that all the Dauntlesses from the *Enterprise* missed the *Hiryu*. The Dauntlesses from the *Yorktown*'s air group, however, chose to await the outcome of the initial attack, and when it failed they concentrated against the *Hiryu*, hitting her four times. The whole endeavor, which began at 1703, lasted about five minutes. Of the twenty-four Dauntlesses that bombarded the carrier two were shot down and three more were badly damaged, one being lost as it tried to land on the *Enterprise*. The surviving Dauntlesses were recovered by 1834.

The hits sustained by the *Hiryu* doomed her as surely as her three companions had been doomed by their hits some six hours earlier. With two taken amidships and two forward, the *Hiryu* was ripped open by explosions that set off a series of fires. The force of the explosions did not go into the ship with the result that the engine and boiler rooms were untouched, and with the *Hiryu* under power there was no question of her being abandoned. The fires nonetheless proved uncontrollable and slowly worked their way to the engine and boiler rooms. With these rooms not evacuated, the *Hiryu* began to lose power after 2123 as their personnel were grilled alive. The carrier was rocked by a major explosion soon after midnight, and at 0315, after the surviving crew had been mustered, the *Hiryu* was abandoned. Some 800 members of her crew were saved, her captain and admiral staying with the ship. The destroyer *Makikumo* fired the coup de grâce with torpedoes, although the *Hiryu* obstinately refused to sink for another four hours.

The Dauntlesses from the *Hornet*, coming late on the scene, attacked the *Haruna*, *Chikuma*, and *Tone*. Six Flying Fortresses from Midway, and another six from Pearl Harbor that were en route to Midway but were diverted against the burning carriers, also carried out attacks, as did six Dauntlesses and five Vindicators from Midway. The latter were committed after dusk and spent their time searching for burning Japanese ships and then for Midway. Ten eventually made their way back to the atoll but arrived after 0145, which meant that neither aircraft nor crews could be readied for operations around dawn. None of these attacks carried out after 1703 resulted in any Japanese ship being hit.

In effect, this last mission by the *Enterprise* closed the day's proceedings. When the *Enterprise* and *Hornet* collected their aircraft there was only one American intent—to put distance between the carriers and the Japanese forces to the west. The only chance of the Japanese retrieving something from the débacle was if they were allowed to fight a surface night action, and this the Americans were not prepared to countenance. Accordingly, at 1915, just three minutes after the *Enterprise* and *Hornet* joined company after having recovered their aircraft, TF 16 was settled on a course due east at 15 knots; TF 17 took up a position some ten miles southwest of TF 16 after 2000 and remained in company until after midnight. By that time the *Enterprise* and *Hornet*, and their screens, were some 250 miles northeast of Midway, and Spruance was prepared to spend the remaining hours of night in that general area. His calculation was that his formation was ideally placed to support Midway if the Japanese tried to see their operation through to the bitter end: the American carriers could strike with little fear of being struck in return. If, on the other hand, the Japanese withdrew under cover of darkness, TF 16 would be well placed to move on the basis of reconnaissance reports from Midway. After the success of the previous day such a policy may have seemed very cautious, but there can be no doubting its general correctness. Its weakness, however, was that it left TF 16 dependent upon Midway for the all-important contact with the enemy, and Midway had relatively few aircraft and was somewhat disorganized as a result of the events of the day. The basic point, nevertheless, was that as dusk gathered on 4 June and settled over a great, and indeed first, American victory in a fleet action, subsequent events were to be determined in large measure by Japanese, not American, decisions—in particular those decisions that had been made around midday on 4 June when Yamamoto had been forced to respond to the disaster that overwhelmed Nagumo's carrier force.

INITIALLY, THE REPORT of the presence of an American formation off Midway provoked a "gratifying current of optimism" among the fleet staff in the *Yamato*. There was no attempt to intervene in Nagumo's battle, no belated attempt to warn him of various suspicions and conclusions that American activity had induced, and no attempt to draw various formations together more quickly than existing plans laid down. The fact that the premise of the whole Midway plan had been shown to be false, that the Americans were abreast of developments and not obliged to react to them, seems to have provoked no second thoughts.

Certainly nothing that had happened thus far in the war could have prepared anyone on the fleet staff for the signal of 1050 from Rear Admiral Abe Hiroaki, commander of the battleships and seaplane cruisers of the First Carrier Striking Force, which reported "fires raging aboard *Kaga*, *Soryu* and *Akagi* resulting from attacks by enemy carrier- and land-based planes. We plan to have *Hiryu* engage enemy carriers. We are temporarily withdrawing to the north to assemble our forces."[3] The signal did not inform Yamamoto whether the carriers had been able to fly off aircraft before being hit, and it was not entirely clear from the signal that the First Carrier Striking Force had been overwhelmed by a disaster from which there could be no recovery. But one matter was clear: if the verdict of the morning's exchanges was to be reversed, the heavy forces to the west of Midway had to come to the support of the stricken carrier force and there had to be a major reorganization of Japanese units with immediate effect. But even as Yamamoto himself was obliged to take charge of the operations on which he had personally insisted and had imposed upon the naval staff, one thing was to become obvious: the dispersal of force, which had been one of the most important characteristics of the plan, confounded all attempts to redeem the situation once the battle turned against the Japanese.

In no case was this to be more obvious than with respect to the Second Carrier Striking Force. If the Japanese were to undo the events of the morning, then this formation had to be brought into the battle with the least possible delay. They needed all their carriers intact, in position, and, in effect, at once. The disaster that overwhelmed its sister formation found the two carriers of this command engaged in operations off and over Dutch Harbor. By the time that these operations could be halted and the formation turned to the south, the Second Carrier Striking Force could not be refueled in readiness for a run to the south until the following day. With its speed determined by its slowest member, the 22.5 knots of the *Junyo*, the Second Carrier Striking Force could not be expected to arrive off Midway until the afternoon of the 7th at the earliest. Such a situation was hopeless if only for one obvious reason: if the Americans were to continue the battle, they were not going to wait for three days and allow the *Junyo* and *Ryujo* on the scene before they did so.

After Abe's signal was received, an obviously anguished staff conference was held on the *Yamato* before a series of orders was issued between 1220 and 1310 that set out the terms of reference of fleet thinking. The first order provided the general instruction for all forces in the Midway area to engage the enemy. It ordered Rear Admiral Kakuta Kakuji to bring his Second Carrier Striking Force south and to join forces with Nagumo at the earliest opportunity, and it also ordered Vice Admiral Kondo Nobutake's covering force to leave units with the transports and take his force forward. The submarines, which had so conspicuously failed to detect the movement of American carriers into the battle area, were ordered to form themselves into a new patrol line in the area where the enemy was known to be.

While it was not immediately obvious, the question of whether the Japanese would be able to turn things around in large measure depended on whether Kondo's units would be able to get into the battle. Kondo was one of those officers who had made clear his dislike of the whole Midway venture, but without waiting for orders he led his formation forward and was able to report to Yamamoto when finally he did receive instruction that his units were moving eastward at 28 knots. The immediate and obvious problem was how long the destroyers could sustain high speeds, but when Yamamoto issued a second order at 1310 a second problem slowly became discernible. The landings on Kure and Midway were suspended for the moment, but with the general order repeated for all ships to engage the enemy, Kondo was told to detach units for a night bombardment of Midway. The general drift of Yamamoto's thinking was for Midway to be neutralized and, freed from the threat of attack by land-based aircraft, Japanese ships could swamp the general area and somehow fight a surface action.

The order to Kondo to detach part of his command for a bombardment of Midway presented problems. Ships so instructed had to be outside the range of attack by aircraft from Midway before making their way under cover of darkness to carry out their bombardment, and they would also have to be clear of the area by dawn: scarcely less obvious was the threat posed by enemy submarines. In deciding which ships to send forward, Kondo had a choice between the battleships *Hiei* and *Kongo*, some 400 miles west of Midway, and Rear Admiral Kurita Takeo's heavy cruisers *Kumano*, *Mikuma*, *Mogami*, and the *Suzuya*, which were nearer. In terms of likely effectiveness there was no doubting that the capital ships were liable to inflict far more damage on Midway than the cruisers, but Kondo had little choice except to commit the cruisers since any attempt to rush his main force forward was apt to leave it exposed to air attack the next day. Such a consideration did not address the fact that Kurita's force was being detailed for an operation without support from Kondo's capital ships and aircraft from the *Zuiho*. Nonetheless, at about 1500 the cruisers, unsupported except for their two destroyers, began their approach to Midway.

Once these orders were given there was very little that any commander, formation, or ship, the *Hiryu* excepted, could do to retrieve the situation as Japanese warships sought to cover the miles that separated them from the battle area. Nonetheless, there were to be two developments that augured ill for the Japanese. First, at 1530, Kakuta replied to Yamamoto's orders with his assessment of his situation and estimated time of arrival in the battle area. The signal, with a clear indication that nothing could be expected over the next two days, in effect marked the beginning of the end of the Japanese effort. Second, after receiving a signal at 1730 that the *Hiryu* had been hit by bombs and was on fire, at 1755, one hour before sunset, Yamamoto learned that the fate that had befallen the *Akagi*, *Kaga*, and *Soryu* had indeed overwhelmed the *Hiryu*.

In retrospect perhaps this was the point when Yamamoto should have ended the whole venture, but at 1915 new orders were issued that revealed that he refused to accept defeat. The orders were to acquire a certain notoriety since they began with the statement: "The enemy fleet has been practically destroyed and is retiring eastward."[4] No doubt it was made for purposes of morale. While the cruisers neutralized Midway, Kondo's forces were to press forward, link up with Nagumo's ships, and then contact and engage the enemy. In a sense, Yamamoto was a prisoner of his own logic, but at some stage reality had to be faced. Once these orders were given, three quite separate tasks—the neutralization of Midway, the linkup of main formations, and the fighting and winning of a night action—had to happen since any one part miscarrying had to mean the failure of the whole: pressing forward to force a night encounter, without air support, threatened to leave Japanese forces to fight the decisive battle on the following morning against carrier- and Midway-based aircraft. Yamamoto's orders of 1915 implicitly admitted this, and when different parts of these intentions showed signs of failure Yamamoto was forced to abandon his scheme.

Failure began to show in the early evening when there were two exchanges, both involving Nagumo and reconnaissance reports. The first, which was sent by Nagumo to Yamamoto at 2130, referred to a signal, received from a seaplane from the *Tone*, which had been timed at 1733 and which stated that the enemy was heading eastward. The second, forwarded to Yamamoto at 2250, referred to a signal timed at 1713, received from a seaplane from the *Chikuma*, which noted an American task force, with four carriers, six cruisers, and fifteen destroyers, in a position some thirty miles to the east of the *Yorktown*, heading westward. The signal contained two such obvious errors—the size and course of the American force—that it is a wonder that it was ever taken seriously in the first place. No doubt the attacks on the *Chikuma* and other more immediate needs explain the delay that had attended this signal's being forwarded, but clearly Nagumo and his staff did not "read" it properly. As it stood, the signal was the best news that Nagumo could have sought because it meant that the enemy was headed toward Japanese forces at the very time when these forces were supposedly intent on a night action. Nagumo's response was to inform Yamamoto that his units were withdrawing to the northwest but would establish contact the next morning with reconnaissance seaplanes. Within five minutes of his having sent his signal, Nagumo received one from the *Yamato* relieving him of command of all ships in the First Carrier Striking Force other than the *Akagi* and *Hiryu* and the destroyers standing by these carriers. All other units, plus the destroyers detached from the transport force, were placed under the command of Kondo.

Kondo, acting on his new responsibilities, issued orders at 2340 that set out a general instruction for all units to seek a night engagement.

At midnight, however, Kondo sent a second signal giving detailed orders for the formation of an extended scouting line with destroyers on both flanks, cruisers in the center, and capital ships held some six miles astern of the cruisers. The problem was that in his first signal Kondo stated that he expected his main units to reach a position in latitude 30° 28' North, longitude 178° 35' West at 0300, and that he would then search to the east in an effort to engage the enemy at night. The position was slightly to the south of the *Akagi* and nowhere near where the enemy had been known to be seven hours earlier. Kondo thus informed Yamamoto that his force was well to the east of where the latter had assumed him to be. With sunrise at 0452, on the basis of Kondo's estimation there was clearly no possibility of his being able to force a night action. With the receipt of Kondo's second signal came the time for reality.

AT 0015, YAMAMOTO ISSUED the first of a series of orders that brought Operation MI to an end. The signal did not state the obvious—that had to await the signal of 0255—but spelled it out in the form of the instruction to Kondo that his forces were to rendezvous with Yamamoto's own formation, the latter's calculated position at 0900 the next morning being given as latitude 32° 08' North, longitude 179° 01' East, or some 2.5 miles west of Kondo's estimated 0300 position. It is possible that having ordered his subordinates into positions from which they could not extricate themselves in the hours of darkness that remained, Yamamoto chose to come forward to share the risks that the next morning would bring. In any event, the 0015 order specifically cancelled the bombardment of Midway by the cruiser force. Yamamoto repeated this order, not that Kurita's formation needed a second bidding: at 0045 he turned his formation back to the east. From what is known of the subsequent position of certain ships in this formation, it would appear that Kurita's was much farther to the east than Yamamoto had appreciated and that it could have undertaken the bombardment of Midway as originally ordered. In the event the only shells directed at Midway that night were eight rounds, fired by the submarine *I-168*, all of which landed harmlessly in the lagoon. Counterfire quickly convinced her commander, Lieutenant Commander Tanabe Yahachi, that such operations did not fall within the proper roles and missions of his submarine, and after only three minutes of shelling, at 0128, the *I-168* submerged and resumed routine patroling.

In large measure the events of 5 June were determined by what happened to Kurita's force after it turned back once its orders to bombard Midway had been canceled. By 0215 it was some 89 miles from Midway when it was seen by the American submarine *Tambor*, then heading south to take up her new position to the west of Midway. The *Tambor*, with the advantage of first sight, found the Japanese ships at maximum range, but the submarines had been warned that friendly ships might cross their patrol lines during the night. No positive identification was possible although the *Tambor* did send a sighting report, but by the time that daylight revealed the distinctive silhouette of the *Mogami* class the Japanese had realized that they were not alone. After they executed an emergency turn-away, the *Mogami* turned back too early and tried to take station not on the *Mikuma*, as she should have done, but on the *Suzuya*. In the gloom the *Mogami* plowed into the stern of the *Mikuma* at 28 knots. Surprisingly, the *Mikuma* escaped with relatively little damage although the *Mogami* lost her forecastle.

When Kurita discovered what had happened, he took the *Kumano* and *Suzuya* back to the rendezvous with the fleet and left the damaged cruisers, with the destroyers, to fend for themselves, their only hope being that somehow they might get under the cover of aircraft from Wake and thereby ensure their own survival. For her part the *Tambor*, obliged to dive when more than two miles from the Japanese units, was unable to close as the *Mogami* quickly worked up to 12 knots. The *Tambor* subsequently surfaced and sent a full and accurate contact report giving the enemy's course. It was unfortunate that this report was not made until after 0600 because for some three hours TF 16 was unaware of whether the enemy force was advancing from the west or withdrawing from the previous day's battle area. By 0600 scouting missions from Midway had found, in the absence of any Japanese formations in the immediate area of the atoll, that the Japanese appeared to have abandoned their operation, but with only ten Catalinas available to search a sector between 250 to 020 degrees to a distance of 250 miles, the chances of contact and gathering of a reasonable overall intelligence picture were not great. What the Catalinas did find at 0617 and report at 0630 were two damaged battleships some 125 miles west of

Midway, making 15 knots to the west. A second report, made at 0700, placed two cruisers on a bearing of 274 degrees from Midway at a range of 174 miles: these were reported to be steaming to the northwest at a speed of 20 knots. The first report referred to the *Mogami* and *Mikuma* and made no mention of their escorts; the second referred to the *Kumano* and *Suzuya*. About an hour later a Catalina noted the presence of a burning carrier, the American aircrew having come across the *Hiryu* in the very last minutes of her life; unfortunately, they failed to see her sink. In addition, another signal reported the presence of two carriers northwest of Midway.

As TF 16 came westward, therefore, it had only reports that were both confused and confusing. With no clear idea of what might be to the west, Spruance chose to go after the force reported to be to the northwest of Midway. The problem with this decision, so obvious in hindsight, was that there never were two carriers in this area, and by the time (1115) that TF 16 came to Midway's longitude some seven hours after dawn, there was no first carrier, either. It was not until 1500 that Spruance ordered his carriers to conduct reconnaissance-and-strike missions. This meant that with the approach of dusk, TF 16 would not have been able to make a sustained attack upon any force other than the crippled cruisers, which, entirely separately on the morning on 5 June, were reduced to sinking condition without any contribution from the *Enterprise* and *Hornet*.

The cruisers were the *Mikuma* and *Mogami*, which were found by Catalinas during the dawn search and then attacked by six Dauntlesses and six Vindicators from Midway. These aircraft, operating at low altitude, found an oil slick trailed by the *Mikuma* at 0745. The Japanese ships were sighted at 0805 and the attack began three minutes later. In the face of ferocious antiaircraft fire none of the attacking American aircraft was able to hit either Japanese cruiser with a bomb, but the leading Vindicator, hit by the *Mikuma* as she attacked her, deliberately crashed into the cruiser, hitting her on her X turret. Flames spread immediately across the whole of the stern and were sucked down ventilator shafts, causing an explosion in the engine room that killed the entire watch. At this stage eight Flying Fortresses from Midway, which had been circling Kure waiting to be called to potential targets, came upon the scene but recorded no hits on any of the Japanese ships.

Perhaps rather oddly, these units were not subjected to attack again during this day, although there were to be three more offensive missions flown—two from Midway, and one by the American carriers. And perhaps even more strangely, American searches failed to find any Japanese formations. Those commanded by Yamamoto and Kondo found one another soon after dawn and linked up at 0700. Kurita, with his two heavy cruisers, joined company at 1155, and Nagumo, with the light cruiser *Nagara*, two battleships, two cruisers, and five destroyers, linked up with the other formations at 1300, immediately after the Second Carrier Striking Force was instructed to abandon any attempt to come south. With Midway launching seven Flying Fortresses at 1320 and another five at 1545, and the *Enterprise* thirty-two Dauntlesses (between 1512 and 1528) and the *Hornet* twenty-five Dauntlesses, the Japanese main formations escaped detection apparently because for most of the time they were hove to and transferring their wounded. Japanese ships saw American aircraft, but with those ships not trailing smoke or white water the aircraft did not see them.

American aircraft did encounter one destroyer, the *Tanikaze*, which had been ordered to return to the *Hiryu* and ensure her destruction after a Jean from the *Hosho* discovered her still afloat. By the time that the *Tanikaze* reached her last known position, the *Hiryu* had sunk. During her high-speed return to formation the *Tanikaze* attracted the attention of the seven Flying Fortresses, which attacked her at 1635 from an altitude of 16,000 feet. Having escaped all the bombs aimed at her, the *Tanikaze* was then found by eleven Dauntlesses from the *Hornet*. The American carrier aircraft were then flying a very deliberate search on a course of 324 degrees to a distance of 265 miles, and when the first of the two Dauntless groups from the *Hornet* found the *Tanikaze* they were outward bound and therefore ignored her. After unsuccessfully searching for the enemy these same Dauntlesses came across the *Tanikaze* as they returned to the *Hornet*, some twenty minutes after the destroyer had been attacked by Dauntlesses from the *Enterprise*. The *Hornet*'s aircraft, attacking at 1610, could not improve on previous efforts, the *Tanikaze* escaping harm other than a near-miss that damaged one turret and killed six of its crew. In return the *Tanikaze* accounted for one Dauntless from the *Enterprise*. The second group of Flying Fortresses contributed to the final attack of the day on the *Tanikaze* at 1845, but again she evaded all the bombs aimed at her. Two of the Fortresses were lost in this attack, one for reasons unknown and the other for lack of fuel. These were the only heavy bombers lost in the battle.

After the *Enterprise* and *Hornet* recovered the Dauntlesses—one being lost as it ran out of fuel even as it tried to land on the *Enterprise* and six ultimately found to have landed on the wrong carrier—TF 16 settled down for the night. With Spruance and his staff having concluded that the absence of contact during the day suggested that there was no enemy likely to be within 300 miles, the decision was taken not to turn away but to steer to the west throughout the night and to conduct a full search, across a 180-degree sector, to a distance of 200 miles. With fourteen Flying Fortresses on Midway committed to search a sector between 220 and 330 degrees to a range of 600 miles, the next morning was to find the main Japanese formations just beyond the American areas of search. The *Mikuma* and *Mogami* were not so fortunate.

The dawn search from the *Enterprise* found the two heavy cruisers at 0502, and the confusion of the previous day was repeated with discrepancies of position and reports of either a carrier or a battleship. The first attack was flown off the *Hornet* at 0800 and reached the *Mogami* at 0946. One Dauntless was lost in attacks that resulted in the *Mogami*'s Y turret being pierced, while another hit in the ship's torpedo tubes caused a series of major fires amidships. But such was the confusion of identity and position that the second strike force committed by TF 16 at 1045 deliberately and systematically searched beyond the two cruisers once they were found and thereby established beyond all doubt that no other Japanese units were in the area. Only then, after 1215, did this force attack the *Mikuma*, hitting her with five bombs that started major fires throughout the ship. A massive internal explosion at 1358 caused loss of power. The third attack, against the *Mikuma* as she settled, inflicted heavy losses among the crew gathered topside. The hits on the *Mikuma* also set off the cruiser's torpedoes, forcing the two destroyers that were picking up survivors to withdraw, leaving nearly three-quarters of the crew of 890 in the water.

Both of the destroyers were hit by single bombs, the *Arashio* losing thirty-seven men and the *Asashio* twenty-two. After having cleared the area on the 6th, the *Arashio* returned the next day to rescue one survivor still in the water; the American submarine *Trout* recovered two Japanese who allowed themselves to be rescued. The *Mogami* throughout this third and last attack was wholly involved in making good her damage, and despite being hit six times in these three assaults by 1515 she was making 20 knots and very slowly drew clear of the battle area.

She was able to do so in part because Spruance was wholly determined not to take his formation within range of aircraft from Wake. After three days of fighting there can be little doubt that this decision was correct, especially because at this time it seemed likely that TF 16 might be committed to the north Pacific. The formation's two carriers were reinforced by aircraft flown from the *Saratoga* on the 11th, but on that day any thought of further operations was abandoned and the *Enterprise*, *Hornet*, and their consorts were allowed to return home. The *Yorktown* was not in company.

AT 0630 ON 5 JUNE a seaplane from the *Chikuma* found the abandoned *Yorktown*. Reported at 0652, Yamamoto's reaction was to order the *I-168* to find and sink her. At the same time the destroyer *Hughes*, which had been left in the company of the *Yorktown* overnight with orders to sink her if her condition worsened or if she appeared in danger of capture, reported that the carrier was still afloat and apparently could be saved. The problem was that while she was being abandoned, her crew was divided between eight ships. Hours were lost tracing and then transferring key personnel, but ultimately a total of twenty-eight officers and 133 men were gathered in the destroyer *Hammann*. Selected to stand by the *Yorktown* to provide her with power, she then refueled from the heavy cruiser *Portland*. Thereafter, along with five destroyers that were to provide a screen, the *Hammann* set course for the carrier.

When she arrived at 0200 on 6 June, she found the minesweeper *Vireo* trying to tow the *Yorktown*, which was leaking over one-third of her length with her engine, boiler, and generator rooms flooded. With the dawn began attempts to cut away certain gun positions and to prepare the carrier for the arrival of other ships, but also with the dawn arrived the *I-168*. She came across the *Yorktown* and her screen at a range of eleven miles, and it was Tanabe's intention to attack the carrier with four torpedoes below her armored belt and on the smallest possible spread. Because the *I-168* would fire torpedoes at a depth of 60 feet but needed 1,500 yards for torpedoes to run true, the *I-168* had to negotiate the destroyer screen held 2,000 yards from the carrier.

After having submerged, the *I-168* approached the *Yorktown* on the basis of sightings every ten minutes, extended to thirty minutes as she came to the destroyers. She passed through the screen as listening posts in the boat noted a sudden silence on the part of American search gear, presumably a thermal layer or oil or debris shielding the Japanese submarine from enemy sonar. The *I-168* came to the *Yorktown* off her starboard quarter and therefore carefully had to move both forward and outward to reach her ideal firing position. Because the *Yorktown* was listing to port, Tanabe's 19 feet was actually 25 feet when he fired four torpedoes at the carrier at 1336. One rogue torpedo ran under the *Yorktown* and narrowly missed the *Benham*. Another ran shallow and sliced through the *Hammann*, breaking her back and causing her to sink in three minutes. The carrier took two hits more or less opposite the torpedo hits of 4 June. Six of nine boiler rooms were totally destroyed and the bottom of the carrier was ripped out. The immediate result was that the ship's list began to correct itself but at the obvious cost: she was lower in the water, the pressure of extra water on her doors and compartments mounted, and at 1410 the tow was slipped as, for a second time, the *Yorktown* was abandoned.

In an attempt to escape, the *I-168* dived under the *Yorktown* and then tried to get clear, but she was caught and pounded for two hours by the destroyers from the screen. Leaking and with chlorine making its way through the submarine, the *I-168* managed to creep away and, after one look through her periscope, surfaced at 1645 at a range of five miles from the nearest American destroyers. Having been submerged for one-half day, in fading light she ran on the surface in order to recharge her batteries and change her air even as three of the American destroyers gave chase. As shells from the destroyers began to gather around her, the *I-168* dived and turned back under the oncoming American units, which lost her at this stage. The destroyers stayed in the area until 2245 and ultimately turned back, thinking that failure to regain contact meant that the Japanese submarine had been sunk. With their departure, Tanabe was able to bring his boat to the surface and then head for home.

The three destroyers returned to the *Yorktown* after their search, but by this stage nothing could be done for the carrier. The light of dawn revealed that the meeting of the sea and the port side of the flight deck would not be long delayed. By 0443 on 7 June the *Yorktown* lay on her port side. Then, battle ensign still at her mast, she turned on her beam ends and settled by the stern. At 0501 she sank noisily as the sea smashed its way through her. Her escorts turned for home.

 Notes

1. Fuchida Mitsuo and Masatake Okumiya, *Midway: The Battle that Doomed Japan* (Annapolis, MD: Naval Institute Press, 1955), 176–77.

2. Walter Long, *Incredible Victory* (London: Hamish Hamilton, 1968), 290.

3. Fuchida and Masatake, *Midway*, 207.

4. Ibid., 211.

5

STRATEGIC CHOICES AND NEW REALITIES

Midway was the first irreversible Allied victory of World War II. The various victories that the British had won in North Africa and elsewhere, and the Soviet ones of winter 1941–42 that for the moment had ensured the security of Moscow, had all been partial or were liable to be overturned by later, more extensive, Axis victories. Midway was different. The loss of four fleet carriers was all but impossible to reverse: indeed, in none of the four carrier actions that remained to be fought during the Pacific war was a loss on the scale of June 1942 repeated, while the implications for future policy of such losses were no less profound. Minor gains such as Nauru and Ocean excepted, this battle marked the end of Japanese expansion and imposed a halt upon proceedings as both sides were obliged to consider their next moves in a situation wholly different from what had prevailed prior to the battles in the Coral Sea and off Midway Islands. To borrow an analogy and to repeat the point made in the

Introduction, the most important, immediate, and obvious result was that the strategic initiative was like a gun lying in the street: it was there for either side to pick up and use. In the aftermath of the battle off Midway, and at a time when negotiations with Britain brought the American high command to the realization that there could be no move against German-controlled northwest Europe in 1942, the high command came to the decision to move against Japanese positions in the lower Solomons. With the Japanese at the same time deciding to continue operations in eastern New Guinea and in the Solomons, the main theaters of operations in the Pacific over the next eight months were designated in the five weeks that followed the American victory off Midway.

IN MANY WAYS the U.S. decision to undertake an offensive in the Solomons was somewhat curious, although any examination of the process by which the American high command came to embrace the southwest Pacific option reveals a logic of events that cannot be gainsaid. The United States in June 1942 sought to secure for itself irrevocable commitments to a landing and campaign in northwest Europe, if not in 1942 then certainly in 1943, and its prewar planning for a war against Japan had never given any consideration to offensive operations in the southwest Pacific, although the reason for such omission, if omission it was, is not hard to discern. In all prewar planning, American naval officers could never envisage defeat of the kind, extent, and speed that overwhelmed the United States and its allies at Japanese hands at the outbreak of a war in the Pacific.

Moreover, the process of buildup of manpower and supplies for an offensive in this latter theater and in Australia was such that no major operation could be undertaken before the second quarter of 1943, although at the time that the battle in the Coral Sea was fought the U.S. Army planners and the Commander-in-Chief South West Pacific Command, Douglas MacArthur, were arguing that in the Pacific theater his command should be afforded priority with its objective as Rabaul. The obvious inconsistencies within such a program were dismissed by MacArthur in his signal of 8 May, which informed his superiors that an offensive had to be undertaken in South West Pacific

Command because "nowhere can [a second front] be so successfully launched and nowhere else will it so assist the Russians." No doubt the Soviets, then on the point of being overwhelmed around Kharkov in a defeat that was to bare the whole of the eastern Ukraine, would have been reassured to learn how important an American capture of Rabaul would be to their ultimate success.

Such a pedigree points to the United States undertaking an offensive in the southwest Pacific in August 1942, and for an obvious reason: if there was to be no major European commitment in 1942, then some form of offensive action in the Pacific in the aftermath of victory off Midway was essential, for both political and military reasons. Militarily, a U.S. offensive in the Solomons, as the first stage in a general offensive in the southwest Pacific theater that would ultimately result in securing Rabaul, was essential as the means of ensuring American possession of the initiative and pushing the Japanese onto the defensive. Put simply, the Americans, having met and defeated Japanese challenges in the southwest and central Pacific, could not assume the defensive and allow the enemy to dictate the next phase of operations both in terms of theater and timing. Politically, with the American high command unable to commit forces to the German war until the last weeks of the year, there could be no question of U.S. forces not being seen to undertake the initiative. In terms of the public's morale, not to mention the Roosevelt administration's needs with reference to midterm elections, the United States had to be seen to take offensive action in the aftermath of its victories. Failure to do so necessarily would undermine the value and significance of those victories.

THE PROCESS WHEREBY the American high command committed itself to an offensive in the lower Solomons in August 1942 occupied only sixteen days, between 25 June and 10 July. This was the period of negotiation, between the Army and Navy high commands in Washington and their consultation with relevant authorities in the Pacific and Australia, that resulted in the directive that gave rise to Operation Watchtower. Inevitably, however, the planning process took a little longer, but not much longer. The first consideration of an American offensive operation in this area was undertaken by the Navy during

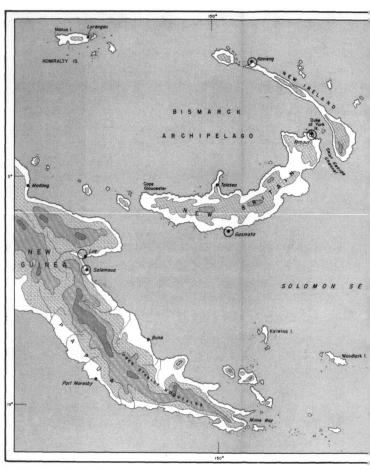

THE TARGET AREA

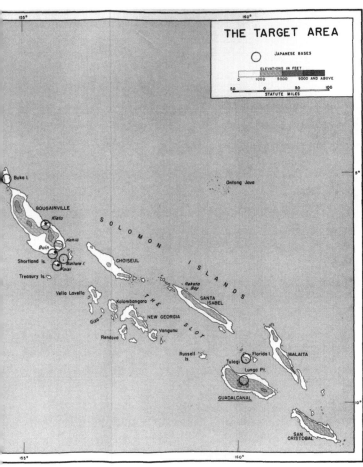

From John Miller Jr., *Guadalcanal: The First Offensive* (Washington, DC: Center of Military History, U.S. Army, 1989).

May in the aftermath of checking Japanese amphibious forces in the Coral Sea, and it took the form of a proposed raid, by a Marine battalion, on the position that the Japanese had just secured at Tulagi. Admiral King was prepared to endorse such a raid, but on 1 June the idea was shelved for the moment because of the realization that a battalion would be too small and that a more deliberate and permanent effort was needed. With the victory off Midway came General MacArthur's immediate bid to make himself and his command the center of attention and the beneficiary of the victory. He returned to the idea of an offensive aimed at Rabaul. With three divisions in Australia available for offensive operations but none trained in amphibious operations, and with likely targets beyond the range of land-based fighters, MacArthur wanted to use one Marine division soon to arrive in theater to undertake the necessary landing and for the Navy to supply a couple of carriers in a series of actions aimed at securing eastern New Guinea and New Britain, these operations being followed by a raid on Truk. As General Marshall explained these ideas to King on 12 June, MacArthur was to be in overall command of the offensive, although a naval officer would be in charge of landing operations.[1]

It is clear that King had no confidence in MacArthur, and there was no doubt that the first months of the Pacific war confirmed his low regard for that general. These first months revealed how little had been accomplished in the years of MacArthur's stewardship of the Philippine Army, and the general's conduct of operations on Luzon, his misreading of the local situation, and his manifest failure to grasp the strategic realities of his own and his country's situation should have led to his dismissal or retirement. Instead, MacArthur was awarded the Medal of Honor and made Commander-in-Chief South West Pacific Command.[2] But, no less obviously, King was no less concerned about what was being proposed on institutional grounds because Marshall and MacArthur were clearly seeking to ensure the Army's preeminence in a theater that was naturally a naval rather than a military one and in which the Army's contribution thus far had been and would be minimal. Thus, for both personal and interservice reasons, King was never prepared to sanction Marshall's demands.

Moreover, it is clear that King had very little time for the detail of what Marshall had proposed: the idea of an offensive aimed at Rabaul, the Japanese main forward base in the southwest Pacific, certainly had no attractions. The problem for King and the Navy, however, was that whatever forces were available for any operation in the southwest Pacific in the third quarter of 1942 could never be more than marginal to requirements, and that any offensive up the Solomons chain toward Rabaul could only be conducted at the price of telegraphing American intentions to the Japanese. At every stage, therefore, the Japanese could be expected to offer resistance to American operations that could never be endowed at this stage with the means that might ensure "overwhelming success." Thus, the main lines of the Navy's proposal took shape in the two weeks after Marshall's discussions with King: any offensive in the southwest Pacific would have to be deliberate, with the occupation of various outlying islands before any move was made against Rabaul.

When Nimitz was informed in Washington on 23 and 24 June of the state of planning for an offensive, he was told that the immediate objective was Tulagi, and there was no reference whatsoever to either eastern New Guinea or New Britain.[3] And when King on 25 June sent papers to Marshall, these referred to forces being "assembled and organized for commencing offensive operations about 1 August with the immediate objective of seizing and occupying Santa Cruz Island and positions in the Solomon Islands, with the ultimate objective of occupying eastern New Guinea and New Britain."[4] The securing of the islands was to be conducted by a task force operating under the Commander-in-Chief Pacific Fleet (that is, Nimitz), and the permanent force of occupation of islands and positions taken would be provided by South West Pacific Command.[5] Not to put too fine a point on it, what King was proposing was for a series of offensive operations conducted by forces from and under the direction of Nimitz, with the Army given the task of providing permanent garrisons to islands once the tide of battle had gone forward. Nimitz was so instructed in the form of orders to proceed with planning for operations in the Solomons and Santa Cruz Islands.

Perhaps somewhat strangely, notice of King's intention did not cause an immediate breach with the Army, in large measure because on the day before King provided Marshall with the papers that he wanted to be issued under the authority of the Joint Chiefs of Staff, MacArthur, forewarned of the main lines of the Navy's thinking, had sent a signal to Marshall abandoning any notion of an immediate attack on Rabaul in favor of a progressive step-by-step advance—a progressive movement—via the Solomons and eastern New Guinea. Such obvious opportunism, which repudiated all the calculations within the Operations Division in Washington and which claimed that everyone else had misunderstood MacArthur's intentions, left Marshall with only one argument: with South West Pacific Command endorsing the Navy's plan the only issue that remained was command. With operations to be conducted within MacArthur's area of responsibility, Marshall naturally sought to ensure that MacArthur would be the commander, but he lectured King on the great difficulty of coordinating land, sea, and naval forces within a single operation, and he noted that "a complication of almost insurmountable command difficulties" would be added by the fact that naval vessels maintained radio silence.[6] To have sought to ensure that operations would come under MacArthur's command on the basis of such an argument revealed just how little Marshall understood about naval and amphibious planning.

With the initial exchanges producing no result, Marshall and King secured agreement in a series of discussions and exchanges of memoranda between 29 June and 2 July, which resulted in the adoption of the Navy's formula in virtually every respect. What was endorsed was a three-part undertaking: to secure the Santa Cruz Islands, Tulagi, and "adjacent positions" with a target date of 1 August; to secure other positions in the Solomons and at Lae and Salamaua, and along the northwest coast of New Guinea; and, finally, to secure Rabaul and adjacent positions in New Britain and New Ireland. Boundary changes were to place the whole of the target area—Tulagi, Guadalcanal, Florida, the Russells, Malaita, and San Cristobal—under South Pacific and not South West Pacific Command.[7] The appropriate instructions were issued by the Joint Chiefs of Staff on 2 July, and King left for consultations with Nimitz while Marshall was left to explain to MacArthur how and why he and his demands had been sidelined. In the event, however, the terms of the directive had not been settled.

On 7 July it came to American notice, apparently via local coastwatchers, that the Japanese, who had established themselves on Guadalcanal after 8 June, were preparing an airstrip near Lunga Point. The construction of this airfield had been authorized by the naval staff on 13 June, two days after Imperial General Headquarters canceled the southwest Pacific operations that were to have followed the capture of Midway,[8] and work began on the 20th. However, it was not until 6 July, when a twelve-ship convoy with two construction battalions and equipment arrived at Guadalcanal, that work began in earnest.[9] On

7 July also, and in accordance with instructions issued by the Joint Chiefs, the commander of the forthcoming operation, Vice Admiral Robert L. Ghormley, who had taken command in the south Pacific on 19 June, met with MacArthur in Melbourne to discuss matters of common interest and concern. The matters, or perhaps the conclusions, that they discussed, however, were not quite as the Joint Chiefs had intended. There was no disagreement about the inclusion of Guadalcanal among the targets, but between them the general and the admiral concluded that the inability to guarantee forces for second- and third-phase operations should result in the cancellation of the first phase in favor of landings in the New Hebrides and Santa Cruz Islands. There would then be a period of consolidation accompanied by an expansion of forces in theater sufficient to allow all three phases to be executed in one continuous movement. These conclusions were signaled to Washington and Pearl Harbor on 8 July.[10]

The reaction, particularly within the naval hierarchy, is perhaps best left to the imagination. Suffice it to say that MacArthur, who had been so insistent on helping the Soviets by securing Rabaul, had first repudiated his own and the Army planners' ideas for an offensive in the southwest Pacific and, when denied command of landings, had tried to insist that a landing nearly 8 degrees of longitude to the east of Rabaul represented an unacceptable risk. Put another way, and a way that was noted by naval planners if not exactly in these terms, the MacArthur-Ghormley thesis was that if Rabaul could not be attacked directly, then the Americans should not concern themselves with targets 560 miles away but should make their effort in the Santa Cruz Islands and the New Hebrides, which respectively were 879 and 1,098 miles from Rabaul.[11] The naval planners prepared King with the obvious lines of repudiation, not that these were needed on 10 June when the Joint Chiefs met and formally discussed the southwest Pacific option on record for the first time. The Army planners arrived with proposals to release more aircraft and transports for landings in the lower Solomons, and Marshall backed King in approving existing plans and informing Ghormley and MacArthur that the Joint Chiefs "had no desire to countermand operations already underway [sic] for the execution of Task One." The two commanders were instructed to concern themselves with their proper responsibilities, which included detailed planning for second- and third-phase operations.[12] The least that can be said about this whole episode is that it is remarkable that MacArthur and Ghormley were not dismissed. Nonetheless, the United States had settled its program for the lower Solomons for the moment, although its intentions with respect to eastern New Guinea were to be forestalled by Japanese action.

In the course of June 1942, South West Pacific Command began to plan for the occupation of Buna in August with the goal of securing an airfield on Huon Gulf. On 7 June, however, just three days after the disastrous defeat off Midway and while the fleet was still at sea, Imperial General Headquarters set in motion the events that were to result in the Japanese attempt to secure Port Moresby by means of an overland offensive from Huon Gulf, a fact known to MacArthur's command within two days. Within another three days, South West Pacific Command authorized construction of air base facilities at Milne Bay. In the second week of July 1942 Allied reconnaissance selected Dobodura as suitable for an all-weather military airfield, and in the following two weeks a planning timetable was devised that indicated that forces would arrive at Buna on 10–12 August and then move to secure Dobodura.[13] But with the Allies aware of Japanese aerial reconnaissance of the area during June, and by early July aware, through radio intelligence sources, that this Japanese effort was to be made under the auspices of the Seventeenth Army at Rabaul and was likely to involve landings in Huon Gulf on 21 July,[14] the Allied intention in eastern New Guinea began to unravel, perhaps somewhat fortuitously.

The Japanese forestalled the possibility of double Allied landings, one in the Solomons and the other in eastern New Guinea, that might easily have miscarried. Under the circumstances, the abandonment of offensive intention in eastern New Guinea was perhaps inevitable, but the inability of American air formations at Port Moresby and naval units to strike at the invasion force known to be at Rabaul on the 18th was more than a little unfortunate, although bad weather was very important in hampering South West Pacific Command's air operations at this crucial juncture. On 21 and 22 July the Japanese advance guard in three transports, escorted by two light cruisers and three destroyers, came ashore at Buna,[15] thus initiating a campaign for eastern New Guinea that began to unfold even as American forces began the preparations that resulted in their coming ashore in the lower Solomons a little under three weeks later.

There can be little doubt that the Japanese effort in eastern New Guinea materially assisted the American effort in the Solomons by distracting Japanese attention at a critical time. Be that as it may, apart from the operations that resulted in the Japanese occupation of Nauru on 23 August and Ocean Island three days later, the effort in eastern New Guinea was the only offensive undertaking in the Pacific by the Japanese after defeats in the Coral Sea and off Midway forced them onto the defensive while denying them the means to fight a defensive campaign effectively. On 14 July the Imperial Navy began its fourth major reorganization since the outbreak of the Pacific war, the first two (3 January and 10 March) having involved forces in Southeast Asia and the third (10 April) having been ordered in readiness for the Midway-Aleutians venture. This fourth reorganization was no more than a re-arrangement of what was left of an already inadequate hand, not least because, militarily, these defeats brought forward the test of a defensive strategy and doctrine with which Japan had gone to war without the basic component of mobile firepower—a balanced carrier task force—that alone could sustain a perimeter defense at the point of contact with a superior enemy. With no commitment to, and without the es-corts needed for, a convoy escort command and without replacement carriers immediately at hand, the fleet reorganization of 14 July was little more than an empty gesture. Such a reality, however, was not very obvious over the next four months.

 Notes

1. John Miller Jr., *Guadalcanal: The First Offensive* (Washington, DC: Center of Military History, U.S. Army, 1989), 9–10. Interestingly, this source, the official Army history of the campaign, makes no reference to MacArthur's signal of 8 May with respect to its Soviet dimension.

2. H. P. Willmott, *The Barrier and the Javelin: Japanese and Allied Pacific Strategies, February to June 1942* (Annapolis, MD: Naval Institute Press, 1983), 165–66.

3. Grace Person Hayes, *The History of the Joint Chiefs of Staff in World War II: The War against Japan* (Annapolis, MD: Naval Institute Press, 1982), 143.

4. Ibid., 143–44.

5. Ibid.

6. Ibid., 144.

7. Miller, *Guadalcanal: The First Offensive*, 17.

8. Ibid., 5.

9. John Prados, *The Combined Fleet Decoded: The Secret History of American Intelligence and the Japanese Navy in the Second World War* (New York: Random House, 1995), 356.

10. Ibid., 19–20.

11. Which would seem to be more or less what King said to Marshall, according to E. B. Potter, *Nimitz* (Annapolis, MD: Naval Institute Press, 1976), 179.

12. Hayes, *History of the Joint Chiefs of Staff in World War II*, 148–49.

13. Samuel Milner, *The War in the Pacific: Victory in Papua* (Washington, DC: Center of Military History, U.S. Army, 1957), 51–52.

14. Edward J. Drea, *MacArthur's ULTRA: Codebreaking and the War against Japan, 1942–1945* (Lawrence: University of Kansas Press, 1992), 39–41.

15. *Papuan Campaign, The Buna-Sanananda Operation, 16 November 1942–23 January 1943*, 2.

II

The Campaigns

in Eastern

New Guinea

and the

Lower Solomons

6

SEIZING THE INITIATIVE

21 July–18 September 1942

When American military planners first considered a direct move against Rabaul, one of the most important single factors in their calculations was the dispersal of Japanese forces throughout a number of bases in New Guinea, the Bismarck Archipelago, and the Solomons. At this time the Japanese situation throughout the southwest Pacific was one of weakness everywhere, although this was of small account as long as the carrier force was intact and retained the strategic initiative: the weakness of individual garrisons and bases was of small account when placed alongside the intention to move against New Caledonia, the Fiji Islands, and Samoa. With first the check in the Coral Sea in May and then the defeat off Midway in June, however, the abandonment of any attempt to move beyond the Solomons meant that the Japanese armed forces had to consolidate their various gains and bring to them the ordered cohesion that would permit their being formed into the defensive perimeter on which they intended to fight their enemy to exhaustion.

To date the Japanese had occupied Buka and Kessa in the northern Solomons (30 March) and both Shortland in the northern Solomons and Boela in western New Guinea (31 March). In the course of April 1942 Japanese forces occupied minor towns in western New Guinea and along the northern coast in order to develop feeder air routes to what would be the main and advance air bases. Fak Fak was occupied on the 1st, Babo on the 2d, and Sorong on the 4th; after the Japanese occupation of the port of Lorengau on Manus Island four days later, the process continued with their occupation of Manokwari on the 12th, Moemi on the 15th, Seroei on the 17th, and Nabire on the 18th. On 19 April they occupied Sarmi and Hollandia, central New Guinea, and nine days later Shortland was prepared as a seaplane base in readiness for Operation MO. The occupation of Tulagi on 3 May completed the process prior to the action in the Coral Sea, but with this check the commander of the Yokohama Air Group at Tulagi, in a report of 18 May that Guadalcanal could take an airfield, initiated the process whereby on 6 July two construction battalions, with some 2,500 officers and men, were landed on northern Guadalcanal by a twelve-ship convoy. On 22 July an invasion force of three transports, without air cover, delivered 1,800 troops, 100 laborers from Formosa, and 1,100 laborers from Rabaul as well as fifty-two horses onto the northern coast of eastern New Guinea around Basabua. Allied land-based aircraft accounted for the 9,788-ton Army transport *Ayatosan Maru*, but there was no serious opposition in the beachhead area: Buna and Gona were occupied immediately, and within five days Japanese patrols had pressed forward fifty miles to secure Kakoda and its neighboring airfield.

In less than a week, and at a time when an airfield began to take shape on the coastal plain of northern Guadalcanal, Japanese forces had secured Buna and Gona and advanced one-third of the way to Port Moresby. As they did so they brushed aside small groups of Australian troops who ineffectively sought to oppose their advance, but by their very success the Japanese were obliged to reconsider their assumptions and policies. The basis of an offensive aimed at Port Moresby was simple: because an amphibious assault had been rendered an impossibility, the taking of Port Moresby had to be attempted by means of an overland assault and by forces locally available. That much was simple enough, as was the desire to invest Rabaul with strategic depth, but the Japanese offensive began in the aftermath not only of defeats but also of the Imperial Army's Southern Army having closed down its Pacific section in its intelligence organization.

That fact may explain, at least in part, why the assault was initially conducted by a force that had been led to believe that the Kakoda Trail over the Owen Stanley Range was a metaled road, of broken stone. In reality it was no more than a track, often no wider than a single man, that climbed to over 13,000 feet. The extreme cold that could be experienced above 5,000 feet was combined with the high temperatures and humidity of the coast, while ten inches of rain in a day was not unknown. Kunai grass, which in various places grew to a height of seven feet, hindered visibility and movement. Such were the problems facing the conduct of any offensive that the Australian command was confident that the Japanese would never be able to reach Port Moresby and that any attempt by the Japanese to move through the mountains would prove logistically impossible. To borrow a saying about another war at another time, the basic Australian calculation was that a large Japanese force that sought to advance along the Kakoda Trail would starve and a small force would be beaten. So it proved, but not quite so simply. In any event the Allies found themselves with the one commitment in this theater that they neither wanted nor had anticipated. Between 10 and 15 July Allied thoughts had turned to securing Buna, like the Japanese by amphibious assault, with the aim of establishing a military airfield at Dobodura. Such an undertaking was to be made between 10 and 12 August—that is, after the American landing on Guadalcanal, which by this time had been set for 7 August.

WHILE IN JULY 1942 the Thirty-second and Forty-first U.S. Infantry Divisions began jungle training in readiness for their commitment to operations in eastern New Guinea, the First Marine Division began training for an operation that the commander of the newly created Eighth Fleet, or more lucidly the Outer South Seas Force, Vice Admiral Mikawa Gunichi, predicted on 23 July. Mikawa, who had commanded the battle and support force in the First Carrier Striking Force from Pearl Harbor to Midway, stated his belief that American troops

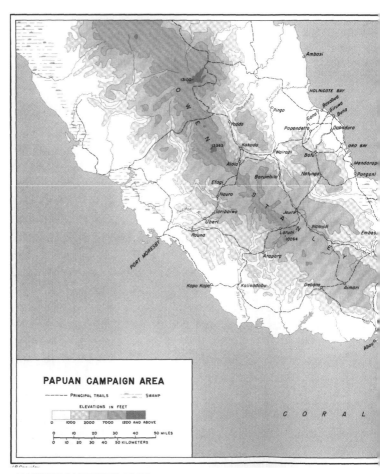

PAPUAN CAMPAIGN AREA

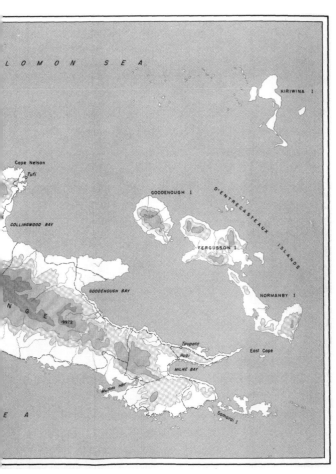

From Samuel Milner, *The War in the Pacific: Victory in Papua* (Washington, DC: Center for Military History, U.S. Army, 1957).

would seize the airfield that was being prepared on Guadalcanal just before it was completed. This prediction was discounted by a naval staff that, like its opposite number, reasoned that the Americans could not undertake any major offensive in the Pacific theater until the second quarter of 1943. The slenderness of the margin between victory and defeat over the next four months pointed to the essential correctness of this basic calculation: had the Americans started with the full and immediately available logistical support that was needed for victory, then that victory would have been won more quickly and easily than was the case. The determination to begin an offensive in the southwest Pacific, as we have seen, reflected certain political realities and interservice considerations within the American high command, and it was these factors that produced the coincidence of Mikawa's prediction and the march of events.

Operation Watchtower began on 7 August when fifteen transports landed the major part of the First Marine Division on the northern coast of Guadalcanal and four transports and four destroyer-transports landed most of what remained of the formation on Tulagi, a small island off Florida Island and formerly the administrative capital of the Solomon Islands, and on neighboring Gavutu-Tanambogo. With the advantage of surprise and preliminary bombardment, the various landings proved successful. The first were made at Haleta and on the Halavo peninsula, on Florida Island, because these commanded the beaches where the principal landings on Tulagi and Gavutu would be staged. On the two main islands Japanese resistance, based on caves on Tulagi and dugouts on Gavutu, was not overcome until the afternoon of the following day, and then American forces moved to secure the neighboring island of Mbangai, Makambo, and Kokjomtambu. On Guadalcanal the Americans were no less successful, the landing between the Tenaru and Tenavatu rivers being unopposed. Some 10,000 Marines were put ashore on 7 August but the deepest penetration inland was no more than a couple of miles. On the following day, however, the clearing of Tulagi and Gavutu was matched by the securing of the airfield on Guadalcanal, the Japanese naval unit of some 450 officers and men, and a labor force of 1,700 men, making no attempt either to deny the almost-completed strip or their own base facilities. Among the matériel captured were hangars that were nearby completed, rollers, mixers, and surveying equipment as well as vehicles, weapons and ammunition, and food. In light of the Americans' intractable problems of unloading essential equipment and stores from their transports, such acquisitions were critically important in this opening phase of operations.

The initial reports from Tulagi and Guadalcanal inevitably drew an immediate response on the part of the Japanese command, both locally at Rabaul and nationally in the Naval Ministry at Tokyo and with the Combined Fleet. The first reports of landings prompted the conclusion that the American operation was a raid or reconnaissance, but the realization that carriers had been committed en masse hardened the Japanese determination to respond immediately to the American move. The strategy of perimeter defense necessarily involved a prompt Japanese response to any landing by the enemy; and with the Japanese military seeking battle with an enemy whom it believed to be inferior, the American operation in the lower Solomons could not be allowed to pass without a countermove. Gathered at Rabaul were aircraft that were being assembled for attacks on the base that the Allies were preparing at Milne Bay, eastern New Guinea, and after 0930 a force of twenty-seven Betty medium bombers (of the Misawa Air Group) and eighteen Zeke fighters (from the Tinian Air Group) and a second force of nine Val dive-bombers took off bound for Guadalcanal. Almost four hours later the Bettys and Zekes arrived over Guadalcanal, but with heavy cloud cover all the bombs aimed at American ships missed while the Vals, arriving after 1500, registered only a single hit on the destroyer *Mugford*. The cost to the Japanese was five Bettys, two Zekes, and all nine Vals, four of the latter ditching while trying to return to Rabaul. On 8 August a force of some forty Japanese bombers from Rabaul attacked shipping off Guadalcanal, the destroyer *Jarvis* and transport *George F. Elliott* both being hit. The *Jarvis* was forced to set out for Noumea but was lost with all hands, while the transport was gripped by fires and became a total loss.

More important, the Japanese raids had three effects. On 7 August they cost the Americans at least three hours as ships dispersed and gave themselves sea room, away from the beaches, and on the following day more time was lost for the same reason, and this when the Americans could not afford the loss of any time given their problems of unloading their transports and store ships. Moreover, the losses cost the three American carriers standing in support of operations ashore twenty-one Wildcats. Although seventy-eight fighters remained available, losses of this modest order persuaded the overall commander, Vice

Admiral Fletcher, to withdraw the carriers at the end of the second day of operations. The decision was one that has attracted much criticism, and in retrospect this decision is hard to justify since the air losses were low and the carriers could have remained on hand with consequences that were to be made obvious by the fact that they were not on station on 9 August.

Nonetheless, one matter needs to be noted about Fletcher's decision. Fletcher had commanded in the battles in the Coral Sea and off Midway, and in what was clearly his overriding concern with the preservation of the carriers and battleships intact he displayed an attitude that went to the very heart of a series of ambiguities that plagued Operation Watchtower and that also affected Ghormley's perspective. American naval lore is full of such rhetoric as "harm's way," but in reality a naval force is never more vulnerable than when operating in support of troops ashore, and that vulnerability is never greater than when the troops ashore are not moving. The keeping of naval forces, and specifically carrier forces, tied to a beachhead raised the obvious question of priorities. If the aim of operations was defensive, to deny the Japanese the means to drive to the south, then the retention of the base was not more important than the preservation of carrier forces. Of course, such a statement raised the whole question of why the base was worth securing in the first place, and an entirely different argument could be used if the base was the first offensive step in a campaign intended to take the tide of war to enemy main bases. Fletcher's concerns may have been misplaced, and perhaps not sufficient allowance has been made by commentators given the slenderness of the administrative margins on which Operation Watchtower was expected to work, but the point was that in commanding the first assault landings of the Pacific war it was very much the case of Fletcher sailing in uncharted waters.

The third and final effect of these raids was to generate an overwhelming self-confidence on the part of the Japanese cruiser force that Mikawa led from Rabaul in the hope of compelling the enemy to fight. Reports from Guadalcanal spoke of ten transports burning off the island, and Japanese aircraft claimed to have destroyed forty-eight American aircraft on 7 August alone. These claims were utterly unrealistic, and they were matched by Imperial Navy reports that the Americans had a couple of thousand troops on Guadalcanal whereas more than ten thousand were put ashore on 7 August. A certain caution was induced because as the Japanese force moved into the Solomons it was attacked at different times by American aircraft, but paradoxically, as it came to the lower Solomons, what many Japanese naval officers believed was an overly optimistic plan of attack proved to be thoroughly in accordance with reality.

The Allied naval formation that had been left to cover the landing area was drawn from scratch from two navies that lacked common doctrine and organization. Moreover, these were days when ship-borne radar was in its infancy, when commanders could rely on operating manuals and still be found to have been unrealistic in expectations of performance. Thus, as Mikawa came down the Solomons chain with the heavy cruisers *Aoba, Chokai, Furutaka, Kako,* and the *Kinugasa,* the light cruisers *Tenryu* and *Yubari,* and the destroyer *Yunagi,* the Allied support formation was divided into four separate forces. Sent to the northwest of Savo to cover the approaches were the destroyers *Blue* and *Ralph Talbot,* while the heavy cruisers *Australia, Canberra,* and the *Chicago,* with the destroyers *Bagley* and *Patterson,* patrolled between Savo and Cape Esperance. Between Savo and Florida were the heavy cruisers *Vincennes, Astoria,* and the *Quincy,* with the destroyers *Helm* and *Wilson,* while in the rear, in close support of the transports, were the light cruisers *Hobart* and *San Juan,* with the destroyers *Buchanan* and *Monssen.* While such a deployment conveyed an impression of defense in depth, the reality was that the *Blue* and *Ralph Talbot* could not by themselves cover the approaches to the beachhead with their radars, while the lack of coordination of movement between the various forces left each liable to defeat in detail.

The Battle of Savo Island, fought during the first two hours of 9 August, proved to be one of the most comprehensive defeats ever incurred by the U.S. Navy. In addition to the *Canberra,* the Americans lost the *Astoria, Quincy,* and *Vincennes,* and had the *Chicago* torpedoed and *Ralph Talbot* badly damaged by gunfire as the Japanese force withdrew; the *Patterson* was also damaged in this action. With the *Chokai, Kinugasa,* and *Tenryu* suffering only minor damage by gunfire, the Allied units were outfought by an enemy that had paid for the advantages it possessed in terms of torpedoes and night-fighting capabilities by years of preparation. The battle marked the debut of the famous Long Lance torpedo, which was vastly superior to anything in the American or British service for forty years, but Savo Island was notable not simply because of a clear Japanese operational superiority to the

Americans at night. What was notable about the Japanese conduct of operations was Mikawa's refusal to linger in the battle area. It was a fear that dawn would bring a return of American carrier aircraft to the lower and central Solomons that prompted his decision to withdraw his formation after such a signal victory rather than to move against the transports to the east.

It was far from clear at the time, but Mikawa's decision cost the Japanese what proved to be their only chance of winning what was to be the Guadalcanal campaign. It was not the case that the Savo Island battle proved for the Japanese to be their best chance of winning this campaign before it had begun. Rather, by the time that the next battle was fought—the Eastern Solomons carrier battle on 24 August—the Japanese chance of winning this campaign had gone. And it had gone because although after 7 August there were to be some fifty or so actions involving aircraft and warships of the two sides, and five actions involving warships on both sides, on 20 August the escort carrier *Long Island* ferried thirty-one U.S. Marine Corps fighter planes into the airfield on Guadalcanal that had been completed and named Henderson Field.

With transports bringing in supplies over the next two days, the airfield came into service with one result that became increasingly obvious with the passing of time. Japanese warships could not survive in the waters that washed Guadalcanal in the hours of daylight, and their attempts to do so became increasingly costly. Herein was the key element that explained the outcome of this campaign, although care needs to be exercised in this matter on two entirely separate counts. First, the Americans' control of the skies over Guadalcanal was the critical element in their success, but in truth the various parts of their effort were all mutually supporting. On the island itself the American garrison was able to withstand a major assault and to deny the Japanese the means of either seizing Henderson Field or preventing its proper functioning. At sea the Americans ultimately fought and won a series of actions that convinced the Japanese high command that the cost of this campaign was prohibitively expensive and had to be abandoned. The air element, which was provided in part by carriers but mostly took the form of aircraft from Henderson Field, complemented these two efforts, and the three together, along with the maintenance of supplies to the island, brought about victory. Second, in stating the crucial importance of aircraft on Henderson Field to the American victory, the critical difference between land-based air power as usually constituted and on this occasion needs to be recognized. In the campaign for Guadalcanal land-based aircraft took the form of carrier aircraft ashore. The air power under consideration in this case was naval air power, and strike capability was vested not in light, medium, or heavy bombers but in carrier aircraft based ashore. The crucial element in victory was the ability of these carrier aircraft to operate and mount successive attacks at low altitude, from which there could be no escape.

IN EASTERN NEW GUINEA in the period immediately after the Japanese occupation of Kakoda on 26 July there was to be one of consolidation on both sides. In the course of their advance on Kakoda the Japanese had encountered an Australian enemy committed piecemeal and not served by secure lines of communication. The capture of Kakoda nonetheless represented what was for the Japanese the culminating point of their attack, and Australian reinforcements on 28 July drove the Japanese from Kakoda. Without reinforcements that alone would have enabled them to retain Kakoda; however, the Australians were driven from the village during the morning of 29 July, and over the next ten days various attempts to outflank the Japanese miscarried. The Japanese response to Australian infiltration or being surrounded was to move forward, and by 13 August they had pushed forward to secure both Deniki and Isurava, forcing the Australians into a general retreat and ensuring the Japanese hold on Kakoda.

For the moment the Japanese had no intention of pushing beyond Isurava, in large measure because what had begun as a secondary effort in eastern New Guinea relative to Lae and Salamaua and as a reconnaissance in force was at this stage being swopped for a fullscale endeavor. An initial desire to secure a report on the state of the "road" to and beyond Kakoda gave way, in the wake of the speed of the advance on Kakoda, to the intention to move against Port Moresby with an overland offensive and amphibious assaults directed first against Samarai, an island off the tip of eastern New Guinea, and then against Port Moresby itself. At first this effort was to begin on 7 August, the day that the Americans at this stage had set for the start of their operations against Guadalcanal, although in the event the loss of the 6,701-ton ammunition ship *Kotoku Maru* to attack by land-based aircraft on 29 July and withdrawal of other units to Rabaul meant that the airfield at Buna could not be put into service, and the start of the main force effort in eastern New Guinea was postponed until 16 August.

By that time, however, two critical changes in the theater were in hand. A major reinforcement of Japanese formations in eastern New Guinea was taking place even at a time when the Imperial Navy put ashore on Guadalcanal an Army formation, the 916-strong Ichiki Detachment, led by Colonel Ichiki Kiyonao, who had acquired a certain notoriety on account of his involvement in the Marco Polo Bridge, or Lukouchiao, Incident in 1937. In eastern New Guinea the arrival of extra troops, achieved without loss despite Allied air strength at Port Moresby and in northern Australia, meant that by 18 August the Japanese numbered some 8,000 Army, 450 naval, and some 3,000 naval construction troops with an offensive intent that the Allies failed to appreciate: the obvious signs of airfield construction in the beachhead area when first detected served only to reinforce the belief that the Japanese did not harbor any intention of conducting a major offensive through the mountains. On Guadalcanal the Ichiki Detachment was landed and then committed to an immediate offensive against the American positions around the airfield by a commanding officer who was utterly contemptuous of U.S. military capacity and who believed that perhaps a couple of thousand Marines—that is, second-class troops—might be on the island.

The result was that in eastern New Guinea the Japanese were able to undertake deliberate offensives that resulted in their out-fighting the Australians on the Kakoda Trail. But their defeat in the action at Milne Bay at the end of August, even as the Ichiki Detachment was overwhelmed by defeat around Henderson Field, brought the Japanese high command to the realization that nothing short of very deliberate efforts, both on Guadalcanal and at sea, was likely to reverse the verdict of these opening exchanges. Herein, however, lay the basis of an obvious problem that was to beset the Japanese effort in the lower Solomons over the next three months. Getting Army units to Guadalcanal could only be achieved by cutting back the forces earmarked for eastern New Guinea, but the knowledge that the Allies had established themselves in some strength at Milne Bay invited a response that could only be staged if Rabaul was denuded of a reserve. Forces earmarked for Rabaul were held at Davao, in the southern Philippines, and in the

Palau Islands for lack of shipping, and in the second and third weeks of August it was far from clear whether eastern New Guinea or the lower Solomons represented Japan's major interest. As it was, with the American landings on Guadalcanal and neighboring islands, elements of the Combined Fleet were ordered to Truk. Among the units sent were the battleship *Yamato*, the escort carrier *Taiyo*, and three destroyers, plus the Second and Third Fleets (the carrier and battle forces, respectively). In addition, the Second Destroyer Flotilla, consisting of the light cruiser *Jintsu* and six destroyers, was placed under Rabaul's command. What this meant was that Rabaul's immediate shortage of destroyers was eased even as the Combined Fleet separately prepared for battle.

THE BATTLE OF THE EASTERN SOLOMONS on 24 August, the first carrier action since Midway and the first of the two carrier battles fought during the Guadalcanal campaign, was a strange affair on several counts. It was odd in the sense that this was most definitely a case of role reversal for the Japanese, who were obliged to consider two entirely separate enemies: the air group on Guadalcanal, and American carrier groups to the south of the island. It was exceptional in that it was the only occasion when fleet carriers fought one another in the Pacific war that none succumbed as a result of enemy attention. Nonetheless, with the American force deploying three fleet carriers, one battleship, six heavy and three light cruisers, and eighteen destroyers in three task groups and the Japanese dispersing two fleet and one light fleet carriers, three battleships, nine heavy and two light cruisers, and twenty-three destroyers in no fewer than five formations, it did result in the sinking of one Japanese light fleet carrier, the *Ryujo*, and the damaging of the American carrier *Enterprise*. The latter's damage control was so effective that she was hit three times but was more or less fully operational within an hour although she subsequently lost steering. On the Japanese side, the battle was notable for the lack of coordination of effort on the part of various formations and for an abiguity of purpose. In no small measure the Japanese plan of campaign revolved around the determination to fight a troop convoy to Guadalcanal, but land-based air formation preferred to offer it cover by offensive patrolling, not close support, while the carrier force hesitated to provide direct support for fear of compromising its own position.

Whether the priority was to get troops ashore in order to set about the destruction of Henderson Field and American air power on Guadalcanal or the destruction of American carrier formations was never clearly resolved any more than Japanese main force formations were able to coordinate their operations effectively. Conversely, American caution, most notably in terms of carrier dependence on reconnaissance provided by land-based aircraft and reluctance to commit air groups to offensive operations, meant that neither of the two Japanese fleet carriers committed to this battle was attacked. The American success in this exchange stemmed from the accounting for the light fleet carrier *Ryujo* and the savaging of Japanese air groups in the defensive fight over the American carriers with the result that after just one strike the Japanese carriers could not continue the battle. One Japanese seaplane carrier and a heavy cruiser were damaged, and the *Mutsuki* was sunk on the morning after the battle in an incident that was destined to become famous. The Japanese destroyer was sunk by a bomb from a Flying Fortress after her captain, aware of the poor record of heavy bombers in attacking warships, chose not to get under way as the American attack materialized. After his ship had been sunk he was alleged to have remarked that even a B-17 had to hit the target on occasion.

The Japanese problem, however, was that American aircraft were hitting Japanese ships on more than isolated occasions. The overture to the Eastern Solomons battle was an action between one Japanese and two American destroyers that left one of the latter so heavily damaged that she had to be scuttled the following day, but thereafter the exchanges favored the Americans. On 25 August the 9,309-ton naval auxiliary *Kinryu Maru* was sunk off Guadalcanal by aircraft from Henderson Field, while on the 28th the destroyer *Asagiri* was sunk and two more severely damaged by a combination of carrier- and shore-based aircraft. On the next day American warships joined the action when two submarines were sunk, one off Port Moresby and the other off Guadalcanal. The Japanese had compensation of a kind in getting troops through to Guadalcanal and in sinking a destroyer-transport and minesweeper (28–29 August), but the torpedoing of the carrier *Saratoga* by the submarine *I-123* on 31 August represented only belated and partial success: one American carrier forced from the order of battle for three months was not the stuff of which victories were made. The fact of the matter was that the Imperial Navy, without including submarines, the transports, and their escorts in the order of battle, committed forty-one warships to the Eastern Solomons action and managed to attack just one enemy unit and inflicted on it no more than en passant damage.

AT THE SAME TIME as the Battle of the Eastern Solomons was fought, the various Allied measures that were to ensure that Japanese operations in eastern New Guinea were doomed to fail slotted into place. By 21 August, Port Moresby had a residential garrison of some 22,000 Americans and Australian military personnel, while the construction program that was to provide for seven airfields in the area was nearing completion. On the Kakoda Trail the first echelon of the veteran Seventh Australian Infantry Division was moving forward to Isurava, while at Milne Bay one Australian infantry brigade arrived to supplement the mixed force of American and Australian units of a garrison that ultimately numbered 9,458 officers and men. With 1,365 Americans present, of this total a little more than 1,000 were service troops and 664 were Royal Australian Air Force (RAAF) personnel. Overall the Allies had the equivalent of a brigade at each of the two airfields at the head of Milne Bay.

Only one of three projected airfields at Milne Bay had been brought into intermittent service by the third week of August 1942 when the Japanese military decided to repay the Americans in kind for their attack on Guadalcanal by seizing the airstrip at Milne Bay. This was to be the first stage of a general offensive against Port Moresby, and it opened inauspiciously on 25 August when one of the naval infantry units earmarked for the landings in Milne Bay was marooned on Goodenough after its landing barges were destroyed on the island's beaches. Another naval infantry unit was able to land in Milne Bay just before 2400, however, and in so doing initiated a battle that was to last until 5 September and that, at its end, represented the first defeat that the Imperial Army had incurred at Allied hands since the outbreak of the Pacific war—the minor actions that constituted "the Battle of the Points" on Bataan in the Philippines being discounted from serious consideration.

Nonetheless, this action has attracted little historical interest, possibly because there were aspects of the battle that did not reflect particularly well on Allied arms. The Japanese landing force, perhaps 1,100 strong, came on shore some eight to ten miles from the three airfields at the head of Milne Bay, and its advance had to be directed along a narrow path made treacherous by weeks of rain. With jungle that reached to this path on one side and the Japanese unwilling to commit naval ships in direct support of forces ashore, there was no prospect of flanking operations. The result was a direct attack that carried to the fringes of the first airstrip but which was halted during the night of 29–30 August. A renewed attempt by the Japanese to carry this position was frustrated the following night, at which point they had little choice except to break off the battle. Almost without food and supplies and wracked after only days by tropical disease, the Japanese began to withdraw the way they had come and started the evacuation of their wounded on 4 September. By the following day all that remained of the Japanese at Milne Bay was their dead, some 600 of the total of 1,900 put ashore. The Australians lost 123 killed and 198 wounded. The American casualties numbered only one killed and two wounded, which hardly accords with claims in the U.S. official history of "the significant part" played by American troops in the first action on 27–28 August east of the Gama River, still less the attempt to link "this first Allied ground victory" with "the first significant American action in Papua." The Japanese were able to withdraw their surviving forces from Milne Bay without hindrance by Allied naval and air units.

The significance of these events, specifically of the Japanese failure at Milne Bay, had immediate repercussions. On the Kakoda Trail the Japanese resumed their offensive on 26 August. With superior numbers and better organized lines of communication they decisively outfought the Australians, who were driven from Isurava, Alola, Eora Creek, and Templeton's Crossing. By 7 September virtually no place of any significance separated the Japanese from Port Moresby: only Menari, Nauro, and Ioribaiwa remained in Australian hands. On 29 August, however, the Japanese forces on the Kakoda Trail were ordered to halt when they reached the southern foothills of the Owen Stanley Range. For the first time the Japanese linked this offensive to events at Milne Bay and on Guadalcanal with an order that stated that the drive down the Trail had to await the successful outcome of the battles in the lower Solomons and on the tip of eastern New Guinea. On the ground, this order trans-

lated itself into a decision to secure and then stand on the defensive at
Nauro, but when the village was taken it was decided to press forward
and to capture Ioribaiwa. This village was taken on 16 September, and
at this point the Japanese troops were ordered to hold this position in
the expectation that the offensive would be resumed in mid-October.
By this time, however, the Japanese offensive on Guadalcanal, on which
so much depended, had been smashed. Ironically, it was only after this
offensive had been defeated that the Japanese command formally resolved that the effort in the lower Solomons took priority over that in
eastern New Guinea (18 September).

AFTER THE DESTRUCTION of the Ichiki Detachment in the third
week of August there was no major engagement on Guadalcanal until
the middle of the following month. In that time there was a flow of
American reinforcements and supplies into the Henderson Field perimeter, the only matter of note being the loss of three destroyers, one
on the night of 28–29 August and two on the night of 4–5 September.
For their part the Japanese lost one destroyer and had two severely
damaged on 28 August, but overall their efforts were largely unhin-
dered as they put ashore, near Taivu Point some eighteen miles to the
east of Henderson Field, the 6,000-strong Kawaguchi Detachment. The
distance from the American holding was determined by a desire for security against attack during the preparation phase: such caution, given
the American raid on 8 September that registered minimal results, was
justified. The distance from the American perimeter around Henderson Field nonetheless imposed massive problems of movement of both
men and equipment. In addition, such distances across the series of
jungle ridges to the south of Henderson Field rendered the task of coordinating offensives from the west, south, and east all but impossible.

The Imperial Navy was also to be involved in this endeavor, and in
order to support the offensives ashore it was to deploy two formations:
one with two battleships, five heavy cruisers, and seven destroyers; and
the other with three fleet carriers, two battleships, three heavy and one
light cruisers, and eleven destroyers. The task of these formations was
to prevent further American reinforcement of the Guadalcanal garrison and to cover Japanese troop movements to the island, the Japanese

expectation being that extra forces would be needed once the Kawa-guchi Detachment had secured Henderson Field. Whether the Kawa-guchi Detachment could break the American defense around the airstrip was doubted by certain high-ranking Japanese officers, most notably Major General Kawaguchi Kiyotake, but there was a genuine confidence that was shaken when the Japanese assault was initially checked and then comprehensively defeated on Bloody Ridge between 12 and 14 September. Kawaguchi, after seeing his force beaten, refused to undertake a second offensive as ordered and was dismissed.

The Japanese defeat in front of Henderson Field in mid-September 1942 represented one of the moments of truth in this campaign. It is one of the unfortunate aspects of historiography that accounts must have decisive moments or phases or turning points, whereas in reality the latter more often than not represent the point when various factors of time and distance, thus far only in the making, manifest themselves on the battlefield for the first time—to the great joy of the uncritical commentator and publishing hack. Midway is an obvious and relevant example of a battle represented by two or three generations of histori-ans as "the turning point of the Pacific war," but if the outcome of this war was inevitable from the time that Japanese carrier aircraft struck at Pearl Harbor, then Midway can only be a milestone on one road, not a signpost where the road divided, and a road that hitherto had led to Japan's victory instead made its way to her defeat.

Nonetheless, this caveat notwithstanding, two matters remain to be defined. The roads that lead to victory and defeat do not negate the need to fight since the battle must still be fought and won, and there still remain within individual actions defining moments. The Japanese defeat on Bloody Ridge was such a moment, and for an obvious reason. The force that attacked numbered some two thousand, and their dead and wounded each represented one-quarter of their number. But it took the survivors a week to get back to the safety of their secure area near Taivu Point, by which time many of the wounded had died and their provisions had been nearly exhausted. For the first time, there-fore, the Japanese high command was brought to a twin realization—that success on Guadalcanal could not be improvised but could only be secured if a deliberate, systematic effort was made on, over, and in the seas around Guadalcanal; and that eastern New Guinea was of little consequence when set against the seriousness of the issues presented in the lower Solomons.

In such a situation the appropriate orders, much belated and overdue, flowed immediately. The Japanese force on the Kakoda Trail was to prepare a defense in depth with battalions forward at Ioribaiwa and companies at Nauro and was to be readied for successive withdrawals. Its priority was to hold the original beachhead area and to await the success of Japanese arms on Guadalcanal, after which would follow the defeat of Allied forces at Milne Bay and then the enveloping attacks on Port Moresby. The Japanese plan was to secure Henderson Field, then take Rennell, Tulagi, and San Cristobal, and move against Port Moresby at the end of November. Leaving aside the operations that the Japanese planned in eastern New Guinea at the close of a successful campaign in the lower Solomons, this reordering of priorities and the commitment of more army troops to Guadalcanal served notice of one very real change between future and past operations. Obviously, army forces would continue to be transported to Guadalcanal, but in greater numbers and in less time than previously had been the case. More important, however, the Imperial Navy would have to commit much heavier units to the waters off Guadalcanal than had previously been the case.

Until this time the occasional bombardment by small numbers of destroyers had been all that the Japanese had deemed could be afforded Henderson Field. But if the air group on Guadalcanal was to be neutralized, and the evidence of the previous month indicated that it could not be neutralized by Japanese air power based on Rabaul, then battleships and cruisers would have to be committed to regular bombardments of Henderson Field—and such a course of action clearly went hand-in-hand with the prospect of more and increasingly important clashes at sea. This change of Japanese priorities was accompanied by a real success at sea in the form of an episode without parallel. On 15 September the Japanese submarine *I-19* in one salvo of six torpedoes sank the American fleet carrier *Wasp* and also hit, from a separate task group some five miles beyond the *Wasp*, the battleship *North Carolina* and destroyer *O'Brien*; more than one month later, on 19 October, the *O'Brien* foundered as a result of the damage she had sustained. To make use again of an old but relevant saying, with the American carrier strength in the Pacific thus reduced to only the *Hornet*, the balance of advantages and the initiative itself were like a gun lying in a street: it was there for either side to pick up and use.

7

BATTLE

18 September–13 November 1942

By mid-September 1942 both in eastern New Guinea and the lower Solomons the Americans and Japanese had reached a point of balance. It was not a balance of exhaustion—that had to wait a month or two—but rather a point of balance because in eastern New Guinea the Allies, and in the lower Solomons the Japanese, gathered themselves in readiness for offensive operations. The military geography of the two theaters meant that the Allies possessed a real advantage in eastern New Guinea that was denied the Japanese on Guadalcanal. In eastern New Guinea a number of different routes led to Buna and Gona, and the Japanese did not have the means to cover every one. On Guadalcanal the Japanese might attack from east, south, or west, but they still had to come up against a cleared defensive position, only some fourteen square miles in area with one flank on the sea, in which the enemy—after the arrival on Guadalcanal of the reinforced Seventh Marine Regiment and sorely needed supplies of all kinds on

18 September—had an advantage in virtually every aspect of military operations other than in terms of the vulnerability of Henderson Field to bombardment by Japanese battle and cruiser formations. The first such bombardment by Japanese battleships took place on the night of 13–14 October, but by then the issue in eastern New Guinea had been decided even though almost another two months of fighting remained before the Japanese beachhead on the Solomon Sea was eliminated.

THE HALTING OF THE Japanese offensive at Ioribaiwa in mid-September, just thirty miles from Port Moresby, served to provide the Allies with a double opportunity: to move against Japanese positions along the Kakoda Trail and to drive the Japanese back whence they had come; and to use local superiority in the air and at sea to turn the Japanese position on the Trail. The first Japanese withdrawal along the Trail took place on 24 September, two days before a concentrated Australian force began offensive operations that resulted in the recapture of Ioribaiwa on the 28th. Three days later, on 1 October, recognition of the changed situation in eastern New Guinea came in the form of a South West Pacific Command plan that proposed an offensive with three related parts: the advance by the Seventh Australian Division along the Trail to Wairopi, the advance of one American infantry battalion via Kapa Kapa to Jaure, and the advance of the Eighteenth Australian Brigade along the northern coast to meet with one U.S. infantry regiment at Wanigela, after which there would be an advance via Embogo on the Japanese beachhead.

The ease with which an Australian battalion secured Wanigela by airlift on 5–6 October led to a change of plan, or at least a change of schedule. Certain of the Australian units that were to be fed into the battle other than on the Kakoda Trail were not to arrive at Milne Bay until the end of the month, but with the 128th U.S. Infantry Regiment immediately available the decision was taken to commit this formation to Wanigela. Most of this regiment was flown into Wanigela between 14 and 18 October, just in time for heavy rains to isolate it from further reinforcement. What was even worse, the plan of campaign called for Allied troops to advance across the neck of Cape Nelson to Pongani. The Australian soldiers, carrying virtually nothing but rifles, were successful, but the heavily loaded Americans were not. Caught by the rising River Musa that obliterated the trail to Pongani, the Americans were halted at Totore on 16 October and then forced to move directly to the coast; once there, they were taken by ship to Pongani, which was reached on 28 October. Unfortunately, the other American force, the Second Battalion of the 126th Infantry Regiment, fared no better on the route to Jaure. Departing from Kapa Kapa (on the coast) on 13 October, it managed to reach and occupy Jaure on 20 October, but nothing could have fully prepared it for the ordeal that it endured in reaching this tiny, unoccupied village. The battalion, which occupied Arapara on 9 October and Laruni six days later, was exhausted by its efforts, and in the aftermath of its march the decision was taken not to move any more units or formations through the mountains.

The situation in eastern New Guinea, in fact, was not so dire as the ordeal of these two American forces might suggest. When the 126th Infantry Regiment was struggling to reach Jaure, the Allied command in New Guinea became aware of the existence of an all-weather airfield at Farasi, which was used by C-47 Dakotas for the first time on 19 October. Moreover, once Jaure was secured, the crest of the Owen Stanley Range was breached, with obvious implications for future overland movement. In addition, on 22–23 October, American forces landed from two Australian destroyers on Goodenough Island. They did so because the Japanese naval infantry that had been marooned there en route to Milne Bay in late August were still there, and as such might present problems for the local coastal craft that the Allies intended to employ to carry men and supplies into Pongani and Embogo. The American move prompted an immediate Japanese response. The Japanese forces on Goodenough were mostly withdrawn by submarines during the night of 23–24 October and thereafter by cruisers to Rabaul. Events did not work out so neatly for the Japanese with respect to contemporaneous events in the lower Solomons.

AFTER MID-SEPTEMBER 1942 the character of the campaign in the lower Solomons changed as the Americans and Japanese made deliberate, concerted efforts in theater. Both sides had been working "off the cuff," but by mid-September they became convinced that improvisation had to be set aside. For the Americans the appearance of the first tropical diseases gave warnings that pointed to the need for reinforcements and to a better and more consistent supply and proper supervision of medication, while the state of the battle pointed to the overwhelming need to get a balanced air group on Henderson Field with enough fighters to ensure the airstrip's security with a force of sufficient size to make real inroads into Japanese numbers.

For the Japanese the situation was more complicated and difficult, and one simple fact illustrates their problems at this stage. By the third week of September, American aircraft had been on Guadalcanal for the best part of a month, but Japanese raids had settled into a predictable pattern. They would be conducted around or shortly after 1200 by bombers that were too few in number to have any telling effect on the air base and that lacked sufficient numbers of Zekes to protect them. Thus, the Japanese were caught in a cycle of costly and ineffective raids, while by this stage a problem that earlier had been wished away began to encroach upon their calculations. The Japanese had to break the cycle of sending reinforcements and ammunition to Guadalcanal in favor of striking a proper balance between reinforcements, ammunition, supplies, and medicine. Several Japanese construction units on Guadalcanal were simply told to fend for themselves with respect to supplies, and in such a development were the seeds of future demoralization and bitter interservice recrimination. Guadalcanal became known to the Rikugun as the Island of Death, or Starvation Island, and with no maps, no reliable communications, no worthwhile intelligence, and no overhead protection, the military's morale was undermined by the belief that the Imperial Navy had deliberately let down the Army. (Perhaps not altogether surprisingly, for much of the Guadalcanal campaign members of the U.S. Marine Corps entertained similar thoughts about the U.S. Navy.)

The Imperial Navy may well have let down the Army, although not deliberately, but its difficulties were obvious. The Japanese policy of perimeter defense was nonsense, involving as it did both the dispersal of forces along thousand of miles, most of which were gaps, and the preservation of battle and carrier formations intact and ready for immediate offensive operations. It took the Combined Fleet more than two weeks to respond in strength to the American landings on Guadalcanal—two weeks in which the Americans were able to bring Henderson Field into service—while there was no disguising the fact that the southwest Pacific represented the most difficult and distant single part of the perimeter defense. Ground and air formations earmarked for the southwest Pacific necessarily had to come from other theaters—some came from Manchuria and China, others from Southeast Asia, but all of them had to make their separate ways to the southwest Pacific by transports. The very remoteness of the southwest Pacific theater necessarily put inordinate demands on shipping both in terms of tonnage and time. From mid-September 1942 the Japanese, in settling upon a deliberate, concerted effort in this theater, which ultimately involved the gathering of more than two divisions at Rabaul from across the whole of the western Pacific, entered into an obligation that ultimately proved impossible. In the final analysis their failure in the lower Solomons was the product of comprehensive military defeat. The Japanese were defeated on Guadalcanal and in the air; and if the balance of naval losses was about equal, the fact was that Japanese victories were becoming less frequent and their margin smaller. Indeed, in the Guadalcanal campaign the Imperial Navy and the U.S. Navy fought one another, and themselves quite separately, to exhaustion, with the caveat that Japanese resources, being less than those available to the Americans, meant that the Kaigun was less able than its enemy to absorb its losses.

Beneath these aspects of defeat, however, was another one that obviously pointed to Japanese defeat in terms of the loss not of two battleships in mid-November in the first and second naval battles of Guadalcanal but the loss in two days of twelve naval and military transports of 74,233 tons primarily to aircraft based on Henderson Field. Here was a recipe for disaster because, as noted elsewhere, the Imperial Navy went to war, having manipulated the figures, with the twin beliefs that monthly shipping losses and dockyard new construction would be on the order of 900,000 tons per year, or 75,000 tons per month. Here were sinkings that represented one month's losses in less than forty-eight hours, but overall monthly losses by this time were running at a ruinous average of more than one ship per day and 132,325 tons per month, and something like 710,000 tons of shipping was tied up in some way, whether directly or indirectly, in supporting operations in the Solomons.[1] By 31 December, Japan retained 5,942,000 tons of shipping compared to the 6,150,000 tons that it had held on 31 March, but with something like 800,000 tons of shipping not in service at any one time because of refits, repairs, and scrapping and with the Rikugun holding some 1,680,000 tons of shipping or 29 percent of the gross total available to Japan, the southwest Pacific commitment and the loss of 75,000 tons in one single engagement could not be tolerated.[2] This second "moment of truth" had to be faced by the Japanese high command in the aftermath of the defeats of mid-November, but in fact the situation at that stage represented an unraveling of the Japanese effort that had begun, if not in the second week of August, then certainly in mid-September.

PERHAPS AS A HARBINGER of what was to come, there were no Japanese air raids between 14 and 27 September. The weather conspired to prevent the Japanese from making the very effort that a concerted effort demanded, while at sea their first attempt to bring Henderson Field under regular attack by warships resulted, as noted elsewhere, in defeat off Cape Esperance. After supply runs on 20 and 21 September that were both cut short as a result of the activities of U.S. aircraft, the Japanese had to abandon any resupply runs to Guadalcanal after 24 September because of the combination of increased American effectiveness in night-flying operations and full-moon phase. Nonetheless, with the Imperial Army and Navy commands settling for a joint effort around 20 October, which meant that the full Army contingent on Guadalcanal had to be on the island by the 14th, the Japanese were the prisoners not only of a desperately tight schedule but also of a significant change of policy. After the failure of mid-September, and even as the Imperial Navy reordered and added to its air formations at Rabaul, in the next phase of operations the clearing of Guadalcanal, not the defeat of U.S. naval formations in battle, was the Kaigun's operational priority.

For the Americans the situation was slightly different in two respects. First, South West Pacific Command managed to bestir itself to the extent that for the first time, on 15 September, B-17 Flying Fortresses attacked airfields at Rabaul, and on this and the next two nights destroyed four Bettys and three Zekes. Such a return was modest, but that was not the point: what was significant was the carrying of the war to the heart of the Japanese effort in this theater. Second, the landing of more men on Guadalcanal, in particular the arrival on the island of the Seventh Marine Regiment on 18 September, enabled the garrison to undertake two distinct efforts. The defense was reorganized with the extra numbers—over 4,000 on 18 September alone—providing some depth in the sense that the term can be applied to a position of only fourteen square miles. Some of the more difficult sections of the defensive perimeter, between the airstrip and Mount Austen, were sealed by barbed-wire obstacles sited to free manpower into the reserve. In addition, the Americans undertook two offensive efforts on the Matanikau, the stream that formed the western limit of their position. Their first attempt (24–27 September) to clear the Japanese from the east bank of the river was less than impressive, but a second offensive (7–9 October) proved more successful. It cleared the Japanese from east of the Matanikau and inflicted the equivalent of a battalion of casualties, but, more important, it disrupted Japanese preparations for the effort that was to be made in the second half of October.

The overall result of the two sides' efforts was therefore a strengthening of both sets of forces on Guadalcanal, additions to the air forces available to the two sides, and a series of skirmishes at sea that began to come together between 11 and 13 October in a series of actions whose outcome generally favored the Americans. The initial one, fought on the night of 11–12 October, was the Battle of Cape Esperance and was the first time in the many clashes of enemy warships over the previous two months in which the U.S. Navy definitely worsted its opponent. Admittedly, in part the Japanese defeat was owed to a certain casualness in their warships that stemmed from the ease of past victories and a lack of intelligence that gave no warning that enemy formations might be off Guadalcanal, but the overall result was clear enough. For the loss of only the destroyer *Duncan* from the total of two heavy and two light cruisers and five destroyers in their force, the Americans sank the heavy cruiser *Furutaka* and destroyer *Fubuki* and damaged the heavy cruiser *Aoba* and destroyer *Hatsuyuki*. Of the Japanese force only the heavy cruiser *Kinugasa* escaped harm, and the fact that the American light cruiser *Boise* was severely damaged in this battle found adequate compensation on the following morning when the destroyers *Murakumo* and *Natsugumo*, having come south in an attempt to rescue survivors, were sunk by aircraft from Henderson Field.

The latter numbered ninety on 13 October. Having mustered seventy-one aircraft on 20 September, the air group on Henderson Field had forty-one Wildcats, thirty-nine Dauntlesses, seven Avengers, and five P-40s by the time that the Battle of Cape Esperance was fought, but, critically, it had fought and won its own major battle by this time. On 28 September the Japanese made a major effort against Guadalcanal with twenty-seven Bettys and forty-two Zekes, but against a defense that had put thirty-four Wildcats into the air the results, for the loss of seven Wildcats, were minimal. The only point that this raid proved, if proof was needed at this stage, was that the Japanese could not afford the attrition inflicted by such a great distance between Rabaul and Guadalcanal. Without any emergency airstrip, any Japanese aircraft damaged over Guadalcanal faced difficult odds in trying to get back to Rabaul, but Japanese attempts to ensure that such an airstrip was constructed on Buin before the end of September was frustrated by weather.

The lack of such facilities was indeed a serious handicap for the Japanese not least because an advance base would provide extra range and time over targets for fighters, but this and other related problems did not seem too important on the following day when the Japanese conducted two raids on Henderson Field and then began an artillery bombardment of the airfield. Such coordination was all but unprecedented and was followed that night (13–14 October) when the battleships *Haruna* and *Kongo*, in the company of one light cruiser and seven destroyers, bombarded Henderson Field. No fewer than forty-eight of the ninety aircraft on the airfield were destroyed. Much of the fuel dump was also destroyed, thus ending for the moment Henderson Field's ability to service Flying Fortresses. In addition, the surface of the runway was pitted, but despite firing more than nine hundred rounds into Henderson Field the Japanese battleships achieved only en passant success. An air raid the next morning (which was supported by short-range Zekes operating from the newly opened airstrip on Buin) added little to the destruction, but a second raid in the early afternoon was met and worsted by American aircraft over Henderson Field. Moreover, despite a bombardment the following night by the heavy cruisers *Chokai* and *Kinugasa*, the Japanese attempt on 14–15 October to carry extra forces and supplies to Guadalcanal ended with three large transports, not having unloaded fully during the hours of darkness and then caught with the dawn in waters dominated by American aircraft, having to beach themselves at Tassafaronga and then being destroyed by aircraft from Henderson Field. The loss of 25,538 tons of good-quality shipping carried with it two lessons: that a bombardment by cruisers with 8-inch main armament could not be as effective as one by battleships with 14-inch guns; and, more subtly, tip-and-run bombardments were not effective substitutes for a carrier force that was able to exercise air superiority over Guadalcanal and its surrounding waters over a protracted period of time.

SUCH CONCLUSIONS POINTED in the direction of the Combined Fleet making one major effort to win air and naval supremacy in the lower Solomons, but the Imperial Navy's commitment to a joint endeavor, with the Rikugun making a simultaneous effort on Guadalcanal, in the fourth week of October merely reinforced the point. In fact, the Japanese carrier force had provided distant cover of a kind for the bombardments since it sailed from Truk on 11 October, but with the Rikugun having been warned that it could stay at sea for a maximum of two weeks it was clearly working to the 20–21 October schedule. Had the Combined Fleet been better served in terms both of oilers and of an awareness of the American carrier situation, it may well have tried to force the issue prior to 15 or 16 October, the Americans having only the *Hornet* task group in theater. On 15 October, however, the *Enterprise* task group left Pearl Harbor, and on 21 October, with the attack ashore postponed twenty-four hours, the carrier *Hiyo* suffered a fire in her engine room and had to return, in the company of two destroyers, to Truk. This combination of events meant that by the time that battle was joined off Santa Cruz on 26 October, the Japanese advantage of carrier aircraft numbers had been considerably eroded. Even more to the point, the Rikugun's attacks on Henderson Field on 21–22 and 24–25 October had both been decisively defeated.

The Battle of Santa Cruz was the largest naval engagement between Midway and the Philippine Sea (June 1944) and the only one of the five carrier actions of the Pacific war in which the Japanese fared better than the Americans and ended with a clear advantage. On the American side were two fleet carriers, one battleship, three heavy and three light cruisers, and twelve destroyers divided between two carrier task groups, with one battleship, one heavy and two light cruisers, and six destroyers separately employed. After the departure of the *Hiyo* and her escorts, the Japanese warships numbered three fleet and one light fleet carriers, two battleships, eight heavy and three light cruisers, and thirty-one destroyers, employed, as was the Japanese wont, in four separate task groups. After preliminaries that saw the sinking of two minor American units off Lunga Point and then of the light cruiser *Yura* (part of a force detailed to bombard Henderson Field), which was scuttled after being crippled by Dauntlesses from her intended victim, both sides found the other's carrier forces soon after dawn on 26 October. Unfortunately for the Japanese, and before the main carriers had flown off their strikes, the light carrier *Zuiho* was hit by a single bomb from a Dauntless scout from the *Enterprise* and immediately forced from the battle.

Although the *Zuiho* had been able to despatch seventeen Vals and a dozen Zekes before she was damaged, from this time the Americans had a rough equality of carrier aircraft numbers despite having been outnumbered in carriers by 5:2 in the original lists. Both sides committed three attack forces from their main carriers. It was the first of the Japanese attacks, mounted by twenty Kates from the *Skokaku* and twenty-one Vals from the *Zuikaku*, that was significant. The *Hornet* was brought to a halt after being hit by two torpedoes, three bombs, and by two damaged Val dive-bombers that were deliberately crashed into her. The second and third Japanese strikes were directed against the *Enterprise* and her group. The carrier was hit twice and also damaged by a near-miss, while the destroyer *Smith* was rammed by a stricken Kate from the *Zuikaku*. Heavily on fire throughout her forecastle, the *Smith* saved herself by steaming into the wake of the *South Dakota*. Somewhat incredibly, in the third attack the heavy cruiser *Portland* was hit by no fewer than three torpedoes, none of which detonated. The last attack of the morning was by the *Zuiho*'s aircraft, the first to have been launched, and these recorded one near-miss that jammed the forward elevator of the *Enterprise* as well as single hits on the battleship *South Dakota* and light cruiser *San Juan*.

For their part the American attacks resulted in two ships being extensively damaged and forced from the battle. One of these ships was the heavy cruiser *Chikuma*, but the other was the *Shokaku*, which was hit by four bombs that wrecked her flight deck. The enforced retirement of this carrier was paradoxically something that the Japanese could and could not afford at this stage. They could not afford to lose a carrier if they wanted to press any advantage that they might gain from these exchanges, but at the same time the losses that their air groups incurred were so grievous that one carrier being forced from the battle was really neither here nor there. Sixteen of the twenty Kates, seventeen of the twenty-one Vals, and five of the twelve Zekes that took part in the initial attack were lost, and in the second and third attacks ten of sixteen Kates, ten of nineteen Vals, and four of nine Zekes went down: in the final attack of the morning no fewer than eleven of the *Zuiho*'s Vals were lost, although all her Zekes were recovered. Thus, of the 139 aircraft committed to these attacks, no fewer than nine fighters, twenty-six torpedo-bombers, and fifty-three Vals were lost, and what had begun the day as task forces with four carriers each with complete air groups ended with two carriers with little more than a single air group between them.

Admittedly what remained was important in that it was the afternoon attack mounted by the *Junyo* with seven Kates and eight Zekes that finally accounted for the *Hornet*. As she was being towed from the scene of battle, she was hit by a torpedo that sealed her fate. She was abandoned late in the afternoon but resisted attempts by two American destroyers to fire what should have been the coup de grâce. Her escorts finally abandoned her only twenty minutes before Japanese warships came upon her, and the *Hornet* was finally sunk as a result of the attentions of the destroyers *Akigumo* and *Makikumo*. The only other major casualty on this day was the U.S. destroyer *Porter*, which was scuttled by the *Shaw* after having been hit by a torpedo from a crashed Avenger.

THE BATTLE OF SANTA CRUZ was similar to that of Coral Sea in that the Japanese had the better of the exchanges but not by a margin sufficient to permit the effective exploitation of advantage. They had sunk one American carrier and forced another one to withdraw after having been damaged, but with their much-reduced air strength they were not in a position to try to do what the Rikugun had failed to do, namely, overwhelm Henderson Field. At the end of their endurance, the Japanese formations had no choice except to retire to Truk. As a result, the focus of attention reverted to the light forces and the continuing task of reinforcing and resupplying the formations on Guadalcanal, and at this stage there was an additional rider. With both

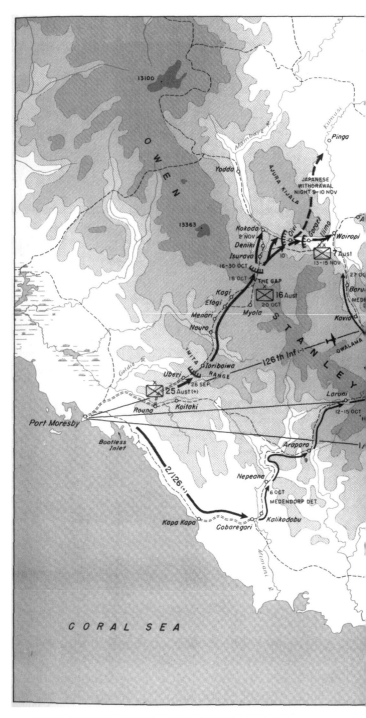

ALLIED ADVANCE ACROSS OWEN STANLEY RANGE

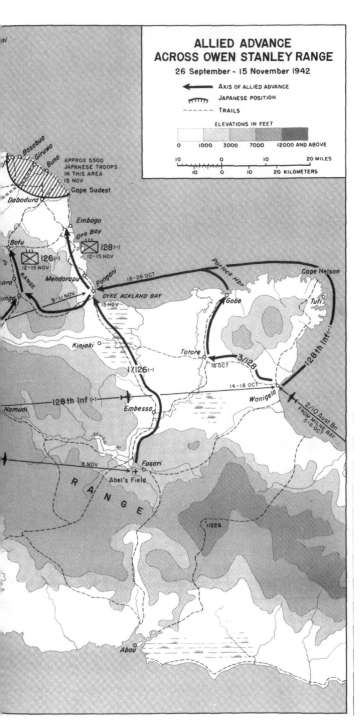

From Samuel Milner, *The War in the Pacific: Victory in Papua*
(Washington, DC: Center of Military History, U.S. Army, 1957).

sides having failed to win a decisive victory at sea with their carrier formations, both sides were willing to commit their capital ships in the narrow waters of Ironbottom Sound. Moreover, by the time that this happened, events in eastern New Guinea had begun to resolve themselves.

The second half of October was spent largely in the preparation of three forward airstrips at Embessa, Kinjali Barige, and Pongani. By early November these strips were completed, and the Australian-sponsored plan of attack was sanctioned on 2 November. Initially it had involved flying single battalions into Kinjali Barige and Pongani, but this scheme was subsequently changed to concentration of forces at Pongani and then moving against both Embogo and Bofu in attacks that would support the main effort that would be made down the Kakoda Trail. These proposals had been opposed by MacArthur on the grounds that any move to Pongani would be immediately threatened if the Japanese prevailed on Guadalcanal, but the plan was then sanctioned with a provisional start date of 15 November on condition that all three forces could be backed by ten days' supplies before the beginning of the offensive.

In fact, events did not wait upon such arrangements. On 2 November the Seventh Australian Division captured Kakoda and its airfield and one week later had turned the Japanese positions around Oivi. The Japanese, for the first time having been clearly outfought on the Kakoda Trail, decided to disengage and withdraw down the Kumusi River valley to the coast and then to Gona, but with the Australians taking Gorari on 12 November and killing some 500 of its defenders in the process, the Japanese plan of campaign fell to pieces. Some of the Japanese were able to withdraw into the Ilimo area but most of the survivors were forced through the jungle to Pingo, from where they moved to the coast and then to Gona. Very few Japanese arrived at the beachhead with weapons, and some subunits had lost men as a result of resorting to cannibalism. With the Australians on the Trail taking Wairopi on 13 November to go alongside the American capture of Bofu and Embogo five days earlier, the Allies in eastern New Guinea seemed to be on the brink of quickly wiping out the Japanese beachhead and ending the campaign in the most eastern part of New Guinea.

In reality, however, the Japanese decision to assume the defensive in this theater had been accompanied by the despatch of construction and field engineer details that had transformed the beachhead. With most of the beachhead area known to consist of swamp, the Allies did not believe that the task of clearing the Japanese from the area would present much difficulty. The Japanese, however, had a beachhead some sixteen miles in length along the coast and six to seven miles deep inland, and throughout this stretch a series of fieldworks was carefully constructed above ground level, with heavy camouflage. Moreover, Allied estimates suggested that between 1,500 and 2,000 of the enemy might be gathered in the beachhead, but the real total was about 6,500, and the Allies had neither heavy artillery nor armor with which to stage what had to be a very deliberate and careful assault.

FOR BOTH SIDES, the immediate aftermath of the Battle of Santa Cruz produced the crisis of the campaign for Guadalcanal. For the American high command, public disquiet as well as the release of news of the loss of the *Wasp* produced for the United States a crisis in the direction of the national war effort that went alongside much more serious crises elsewhere, most obviously around Stalingrad and at Alamein. For the Japanese the failure of the Second Infantry Division's assault pointed to two priorities, namely, the despatch of another division to Guadalcanal, and the final resolving of supply problems. The time when such self-evident needs could be realized effectively had passed because the sending of a second division to Guadalcanal would not have the effect of strengthening Japanese forces on the island but of covering losses, and only at the price of exacerbating supply problems. With the advantage of hindsight, it can be seen that the need for a second division was before, not after, the October attack, when what had been needed for success had been two widely separated assaults in strength. As it was, reports in U.S. newspapers that American counterattacks were clearing the Japanese from positions within the perimeter fortified the belief in Tokyo of the narrowness of the margin by which victory had eluded Japanese arms. But with a division's supply needs assessed at 200 tons per day or five destroyer loads per night, and the assessment that getting an extra 30,000 troops from two or so divisions plus their supplies to Guadalcanal would require the services of fifty transports or 800 destroyer and twenty seaplane carrier runs, the obvious difficulties facing the Japanese in trying to maintain just one division on Guadalcanal, still less twice that number, need no elaboration. A minimum commitment of five destroyers per night every night clearly had to abandon any pretense or element of surprise but would obviously be exposed to American air power on Henderson Field and to submarine or surface ship attack.

What, in effect, had happened was that for all their efforts in September and October the Japanese had been able to do no more than match the growth of American numbers on Guadalcanal. Even when the Imperial Navy finally did inflict such losses on the U.S. carrier groups, the Japanese forces were still not able to dominate the lower Solomons because the Kaigun could not curb Henderson Field and the Rikugun could not overrun a perimeter defense and airfield that between them mustered a garrison force of 23,088 American military personnel on Guadalcanal on 13 October, and that received significant artillery reinforcement around the end of the month. The reality of the situation, hidden from both sides, was that if the Japanese could not prevail on, off, and over Guadalcanal in the last week of October after the immense effort undertaken over the previous four weeks, then they were never going to do so; and after the failure of the attack on Henderson Field, the Japanese would have been well advised to cut their losses. Wars, campaigns, and battles, however, do not unfold in so logical and neat a way, even if in terms of timing the issue on Guadalcanal was finally seen to be resolved as Australian and American troops gathered to surround and destroy the Buna-Gona beachhead.

 Notes

1. Mark Parillo, *The Japanese Merchant Fleet in World War II* (Annapolis, MD: Naval Institute Press, 1993), 78.

2. Ibid., 76.

8

DECISION

26 October–31 December 1942

The seventeen days that followed the end of the battle of Santa Cruz were perhaps the most complicated and confusing of the whole campaign in the lower Solomons. In a campaign on Guadalcanal that was notable for American success in fighting from fixed positions, there was considerable movement. At sea there was a virtual shuttle service of men and supplies by the Kaigun that was dubbed "the Tokyo Express" by the Americans, and in the air there were changes involving formations and individuals on both sides. At the highest levels, in national capitals, and in theater, there were deliberations and decisions that reflected the seriousness of the situation, and there was also the simple fact that these levels of command were brought face to face with the desperate reality of the situation on and over Guadalcanal. The chief of the Operations Division of the Army General Staff, Colonel Hattori Takushiro, after a matter of hours on the island, recorded the view that the Japanese situation was "beyond

imagination,"* but one conclusion that he drew was significant. He reported to Tokyo that the forces already on Guadalcanal could be dis-
regarded in terms of offensive capability, and in submitting such a
report Hattori summarized the trend of events in this period. These
generally worked to the detriment of Japanese forces, which were considerably weaker by mid-November than they had been even at the end
of the failed attack in October.

With the advantage of hindsight, it is possible to argue that this was
the time for the Japanese to have abandoned the fight for the island.
But in a real sense by this stage of proceedings, the Imperial Navy and
Army had become prisoners of their own beliefs. Guadalcanal, more
for the Navy than the Army but for both services, had become the
battle that was sought, and it was to be the decisive battle where American will was to be broken. Thus the battle could not be suspended. In
fact, however, it was not the battle that the interwar Kaigun had
planned to fight. In the lower Solomons it was the American offensive,
not the Japanese defense, that had control of the airfield and thus local air superiority, and the Imperial Navy was thus obliged to labor
under the very conditions that it had anticipated would break the
Americans. This critical point of difference eluded the Imperial Navy
in the last quarter of 1942 with the result that it prepared to make an
ever greater effort to win this particular campaign. In a sense, the situation that was in the process of manifesting itself was one that the Imperial Navy could never have recognized. In the interwar period it
prepared itself, in terms of doctrine, weaponry, and ship construction,
to fight the battle it planned to win, but this translated itself differently
to the point that the Imperial Navy was only able to fight the battle it
planned to win. At this time, October-November 1942, the only battle
it could win was the one it planned to fight. Unfortunately for the
Kaigun, the battle that presented itself was not one that the Imperial
Navy had anticipated.

IN THE IMMEDIATE AFTERMATH of the Battle of Santa Cruz, Japanese joint service planning selected 13 November as the date when the

---

*Richard B. Frank, *Guadalcanal* (New York: Random House, 1990), 417.

final successful offensive would begin. The basis of this schedule, which was finally settled no more than twenty-four hours before its first part was to be implemented, was for major reinforcement of the garrison on Guadalcanal preceded by three days of intense operations by land-based air formations at Rabaul and Buin that were intended to seize air superiority from the Americans. With support and covering formations to the north, the battleships *Hiei* and *Kirishima* were to pound Henderson Field on the night before the various transports arrived at Guadalcanal to discharge their troops and, critically, supplies for twenty days. With these shipments heavy in terms of long-range naval guns and shells, the Japanese calculated that land-based artillery would have to neutralize Henderson Field, and then another major convoy would bring to the island the troops needed to overrun the American positions around the airfield.

In devising this plan, three matters seemed to possess singular significance. First, although the various air formations at Rabaul and Buin by this stage numbered an unprecedented 158 aircraft, with 125 operational, clearly neither Japanese service was prepared to place its trust in being able to neutralize the American formations using the three strips that by now went under the single name of Henderson Field. Second, the Imperial Navy did not believe that naval bombardment could neutralize Henderson Field for more than two days, and in any event it planned to have the battleship bombardment supplemented on the following night by a bombardment by cruisers. Third, the logic behind this last arrangement is elusive. If a cruiser bombardment could not be as effective as one carried out by capital ships, then reason would seem to suggest that either more than two capital ships should be committed to any single bombardment or two different battleships should be committed to bombardments on successive nights. It was not that the Combined Fleet was short of battleships at Truk, and apparently, in October, Yamamoto seriously considered taking the newly commissioned *Yamato* and *Musashi* against Henderson Field, though given that they had nothing other than armor-piercing rounds for their main armament, what they might have achieved is highly questionable. Moreover, with the Imperial Navy genuinely believing that it had sunk four carriers and one battleship at Santa Cruz, it clearly had both the opportunity and the numerical advantage to increase the scale and intensity of operations in a manner of its own choosing. What the Imperial Navy did, in effect, was to commit its formations on a scale that was too small to be effective and liable to defeat while the greater part of its strength was held in the general support and cover roles.

Further, to these matters must be added another. By this stage of proceedings, the Kaigun had come to favor fighting large convoys, well spaced in terms of time, rather than more frequent, smaller convoys to Guadalcanal. In terms of a host of naval calculations, the basis of this one may be obvious, but the fact was that in the few hours of darkness, available individual transports from large convoys might not be more than one-third unloaded before it was time to leave the landing beaches. In other words, the Imperial Navy, by putting its own administrative priorities first, subordinated the operational priorities of the Army ashore to its own program and requirements. The reality was that events on Guadalcanal had to dictate timetables and schedules to which naval formations and units conformed. Lest such comment be regarded as criticism either ill founded or exaggerated, a double caveat needs to be noted. Operational priorities should determine administrative arrangements, but what is operationally sought must always be within the bounds of what is administratively possible. But such was the state of the Army formations on Guadalcanal in the wake of the defeat in the fourth week of October 1942 that one must doubt if there was anything that the Imperial Navy could have done at this stage to reverse the disastrous state of affairs that prevailed.

THE IMPERIAL ARMY FORMATIONS had been reduced to a perilous state in part because of the inadequacy of its lines of communication but also because by the beginning of November the American effort, which had been run on a shoestring, had finally assumed ownership of a logistical base sufficient to ensure success. This base did not present the theater command with any marked advantage and its most serious weakness was lack of shipping, but the critical point was that the American line of communication to its forces on Guadalcanal was more substantial than and not as exposed to loss as its Japanese counterpart. As a result, the immediate aftermath of victory in late October 1942 saw a rotation of air formations and personnel on Guadalcanal and the movement of reinforcements to Lunga Point that for the first time allowed the Americans to assume major offensive operations.

In the first week of November the Americans undertook an offensive over the Matanikau with the intention of securing Kokumbona and clearing the Japanese from positions east of the River Poha. This plan was designed to deprive the Japanese of their landing area around Kokumbona and their firebases from which the airstrips of Henderson Field had been brought under artillery attack. As this offensive ripped open a weakened Japanese defense that mustered two wrecked regiments to hold the line from the Matanikau to Mount Austen, the Americans chose to strengthen their forces on the eastern side of Henderson Field in order to wreck Japanese preparations around Koli Point, where Japanese forces were known to be concentrating. With the Japanese formations in this sector being built up in readiness for an offensive in late December, the Americans possessed advantages of numbers and cohesion here. The result was to be appreciable American successes both to the west (30 October–3 November) and to the east (3–4 November) of Henderson Field, but in both sectors comprehensive victories proved elusive. In the west the Americans had numbers sufficient only to clear the coastal sector, while in the east they were successful in disrupting Japanese preparations but only at an unexpected price: the Shoji Detachment in this sector chose after 12 November to seek to link up with forces to the west. Its march to the west was to take until 4 December in which time the Japanese columns were relentlessly harassed by one Marine battalion, Carlson's Raiders. An estimated 3,000 Japanese started from the Tetere area but had been reduced to about 1,300 when the Lunga was reached on 20 November. About 800 survived to join the Japanese formations to the west, but only an estimated twenty or thirty men were in any condition to fight. The Raiders lost sixteen killed and claimed to have killed about 500 Japanese soldiers in the course of this movement through and fighting in the jungle.

While the battle in the east was unfolding to their advantage, the Americans in the western sector paused to clear areas and to bring fresh units, primarily from the 164th Infantry Regiment, into positions from which to resume the offensive. On 10 November the advance on Kokumbona was resumed, but progress was very slow in large measure because Japanese reinforcements had been ferried into Kokumbona in the meantime. On the following afternoon, however, the advance was abandoned and units were ordered to retire behind the Matanikau. The withdrawal was completed the next day (12 November), with a sense of mystification engulfing the units and formations involved. In one obvious sense, the cause of this withdrawal had been telegraphed by the number and intensity of the Japanese air raids of 10 and 11 November. Clearly what was happening was that the Japanese were about to make their main effort. Coast-watchers in the upper Solomons warned of some sixty-one Japanese ships, including thirty-three destroyers, being held off Shortland, but by 9–10 November the American high command knew of the enemy's intentions, virtually chapter and verse, and were aware that the main Japanese effort would be made on the 13th, a Friday. The Americans had not been able to recover the information that two battleships would conduct a bombardment of Henderson Field as part of this undertaking, but they knew about everything else. Checking the offensive beyond the Matanikau clearly represented a consolidation of success pending the outcome of this next Japanese effort.

These days in eastern New Guinea saw the noose slowly begin to tighten around the Japanese and their beachhead. With American forces available in numbers for the first time, the sea route to Pongani secure, and the Fifth U.S. Air Force mustered in strength sufficient to maintain formations north of the Owen Stanley Range, South West Pacific Command planned to mount a two-division attack on both banks of the Girua with the aim of splitting the Japanese position in two. The main American effort east of the Girua was to be made from the Dobodura area against Buna Mission and the old airstrip near the Duropa Plantation, the latter effort being supported by American forces moving along the coast from Embogo.

Neither South West Pacific Command (that is, MacArthur and his acolytes) nor the greater part of the Thirty-second U.S. Infantry Division expected serious resistance, and at first it seemed that their confidence was justified. The attack opened on 16 November, and within two days the Australians had advanced almost to Gona while the Americans secured Soputa on the 21st and then moved against Sanananda. On the coast, however, the American advance faltered, in large measure because the attempt to transport heavy equipment in luggers fell afoul of Japanese aircraft, while around Buna the Japanese had prepared positions that channeled American advances and left each one vulnerable to defeat. Japanese field positions were mutually supporting; many had no forward-facing positions but had fire positions to the flank and rear and were in any event sited in depth and in a way that permitted their being manned successively despite numerical weakness. The Australians fought their way into Gona only to be forced out, but elsewhere the Allied attacks stalled amid bitter recriminations that demonstrated that allies are not necessarily friends. By the end of November the Allied advances had stalled and the Japanese continued to hold their beachhead area intact.

In such a situation there was the search for scapegoats and inevitable dismissals demanded by MacArthur, who arrived in New Guinea on 6 November from his headquarters at Melbourne. In the event, the various changes did not matter a great deal: the problem lay in lack of heavy artillery or tank support for troops who were exhausted, starved, and clothed in rags. The inroads of tropical diseases into formation strengths were such that by December certain Australian units had recorded total casualties of more than 100 percent (individuals had been hospitalized more than once), and the Australians refused to recognize malaria as an illness. Perhaps not surprisingly, therefore, the first attempt to mount a deliberate set-piece assault on the Japanese beachhead fell apart almost as soon as it began on 5 December. Remarkably, despite fighting in swamps that reached armpit level and against fieldworks that often could not be seen until a matter of yards away, the Australians were able to secure Gona on 9 December, and on 14 December a battalion from the 128th Infantry Regiment took Buna village, forcing the Japanese to reconstitute their positions in this sector around Buna Mission. In securing Gona and overcoming Japanese resistance in this area the Australians captured the all-important anchorage at Basabua, where the enemy had come ashore some five months earlier, but in spite of this loss some 1,300 Japanese troops were put ashore during December in a last vain attempt to hold onto the beachhead. It was not until 2 January 1943 that American forces finally overran Buna, but the outcome of the campaign was never in doubt from the time that the final offensive from Wairopi began in mid-November.

THUS, ONE RETURNS TO the lower Solomons in order to provide an account of the episodes that resolved the issue of victory and defeat in the southwest Pacific theater at this time, and rightly so. The two naval battles of Guadalcanal possess singular significance and are so different in terms of dramatic quality and finality from any of the other naval actions in this campaign that they can only be compared with one another. Their real significance, however, lies not in comparison but in considering their having complemented one another. In so doing they forced the Japanese to recognize final defeat in the lower Solomons.

The two actions that decided the Guadalcanal campaign were the first and second naval battles of Guadalcanal, 12–13 November and 14–15 November, respectively. The second of these two battles was one of only two occasions in the Pacific war when capital ships engaged one another, and was one of only three battles in the Second World War which saw the sinking of capital ships in night actions. The two actions off Guadalcanal in November 1942 therefore are in very select company, as befits their status as rare examples when individual actions decided a much larger campaign. Naval history is plagued by the mythology of "the decisive battle," when in reality the evidence points to the protracted nature of naval warfare and the infrequency of major fleet actions. Here, however, were two naval actions that unusually were fought to a finish, in the case of the first battle almost literally.

The two actions arose from the Japanese determination to bring fresh troops to Guadalcanal in readiness for a third major offensive against Henderson Field in December. During the night of 12–13 November the American airstrips were to be subjected to naval bombardment by the capital ships *Hiei* and *Kirishima*, which were to be screened by the light cruiser *Nagara* and fourteen destroyers drawn from at least four different formations. The Americans, however, were involved in bringing three transports into Guadalcanal on 11 November, and with the gathering of covering forces in the waters north of the island on the following day the transports and damaged warships were withdrawn and a force consisting of two heavy and two light cruisers and eight destroyers was raised with the intention of meeting the enemy between Savo and Lunga Point.

By general consent, the terms of reference of the action that was fought in the early hours of 13 November were provided by a certain Japanese laxness and failure to observe proper precautions. The Battle of Cape Esperance had been the first and only occasion in which the Americans sank a Japanese warship in a night action, and it certainly does not seem to have overly concerned a Kaigun secure in its own conceit and its own sense of superiority in this type of operation. On

13 November, however, the Americans caught the Japanese task group not deployed operationally and not at readiness. The result was that with the advantage of radar and first sighting, the Americans quickly found themselves in contact with the enemy at ranges where torpedoes did not have running time in which to arm themselves and where battleship main armament could not be depressed sufficiently to engage the enemy. Thus ensued one of the most ferocious naval actions of the entire Second World War, and if one seeks a parallel action, one has to settle for that of 1 November 1943 in which the American destroyer *Borie* and German submarine *U-405* rammed, attempted to board, and finally sank one another in the North Atlantic.

Almost one year earlier, in an assault that lasted just thirty-eight minutes, three ships were sunk outright, but the toll of ships disabled or left sinking ultimately meant that the Americans lost the light cruiser *Atlanta* and destroyers *Laffey*, *Barton*, *Cushing*, and *Monssen*. The damaged light cruiser *Juneau* was sunk the next day by the Japanese submarine *I-26*, and the heavy cruisers *San Francisco* and *Portland* and the destroyers *Aaron Ward* and *Sterett* were badly damaged. With the light cruiser *Helena* sustaining only minor damage, only two U.S. destroyers emerged unscathed from this action. On the Japanese side the destroyers *Akatsuki* and *Yudachi* were sunk and two other destroyers, the *Amatsukaze* and *Ikazuchi*, were damaged perhaps more seriously than is usually acknowledged. Critically, the capital ship *Hiei* was hit more than eighty times during the night action. Her steering compartments were wrecked, and she was caught the next day by a series of attacks by carrier aircraft from the *Enterprise*, aircraft from Henderson Field, and B-17 Flying Fortresses from Espiritu Santo. Some twenty-eight Dauntlesses, twenty-eight Avengers, and fourteen Flying Fortresses descended on the *Hiei* during the day, allegedly hitting her with three or more bombs and four or more torpedoes. After much dispute between her admiral and captain, the *Hiei* was abandoned in the late afternoon and sank unobserved some time during the next night.

The Japanese capacity to overstate the losses inflicted on the enemy seems in the course of the Pacific war to have been inversely related to reality. Time after time one reads vastly inflated claims that never seem to have been subjected to critical analysis but were readily accepted. Thus, this action cost the Americans five heavy and two light cruisers and eight destroyers, with another two cruisers and six destroyers damaged to some degree, and on the basis of such figures the Japanese could claim overall success even though the capital ships had failed to conduct a bombardment of Henderson Field. The latter, of course, was far more important to the Japanese than a mere head count with respect to losses because one convoy had to be brought to Guadalcanal. It was ordered to return to the upper Solomons while Japanese forces and plans were recast to provide for a naval bombardment on the next night (13–14 November) by the *Kirishima* and heavy cruisers *Atago* and *Takao*. There appears to have been no thought of the *Haruna* and *Kongo* being detached for this particular task, though given the fact that they were attached to the carrier force (with the *Hiyo* and *Junyo*), this is perhaps not altogether surprising. For the Americans there was basically only one decision to be made. The burden of the defense had to be met by the *Enterprise* and the air group on Henderson Field during the hours of daylight, but with the destruction of the formations that had covered Ironbottom Sound the question was whether the battleships *South Dakota* and *Washington* should be committed to these waters and to the defense of Henderson Field at night. The decision was that they, and four destroyers, should be thus committed, but the decision was so difficult and took so long that there could be no possibility of this new formation being in position for the next night. The earliest that it could be in place would be during the night of 14–15 November.

During the night of 13–14 November, however, the heavy cruisers *Maya* and *Suzuya*, with an escort of one light cruiser and four destroyers, conducted a thirty-one-minute bombardment of Henderson Field. Covered by one light and two heavy cruisers that did not take any part in the attempt to neutralize the airfield, the *Maya* and *Suzuya* managed to miss the main airstrip. The second strip was bombarded and two Wildcats and one Dauntless were destroyed, but inevitably the price for such inaccuracy was to be paid by the troop convoy, consisting of eleven transports and twelve escorts, that sailed from Shortland just around sunset on the 13th. Successive attacks on the following day accounted first for the veteran heavy cruiser *Kinugasa* off Rendova (with three more cruisers damaged and forced to withdraw from the battle), and then 20,784 tons of shipping: the Navy transport *Canberra Maru* and Army transport *Nagara Maru* were both sunk, while the *Sado Maru* was damaged and forced to return to Shortland in the company of two destroyers. The depleted convoy then lost the Army transport

Brisbane Maru (5,415 tons), and then two more—the Navy transport *Arizona Maru* (9,683 tons) and Army transport *Shinanogawa Maru* (7,504 tons)—before the final attack of the day accounted for one last transport, the Army's 7,145-ton *Nako Maru*. Japanese destroyers picked up more than 5,000 troops from the sea, but the rescue of such numbers could not disguise the fact that Japanese formation and unit cohesion had been lost along with the transports, supplies, and heavy equipment. With just four transports left to make their way to Guadalcanal under cover of darkness, the American success on this day against shipping must have ended any possibility of the Japanese being able to put together any major offensive undertaking on Guadalcanal during December. Japanese shore-based air formations managed to mount only thirty-six Zeke missions in defense of the convoy, while the carrier force appears to have made no real effort either to neutralize a frenetically busy Henderson Field or to provide a proper cover for the troop convoy.

What various Japanese search planes did note on the afternoon of 14 November, however, was a task group to the south of Guadalcanal. Different reports credited this group with different types of warships, but it seems that there emerged a consensus with the Combined Fleet staff that this formation included cruisers and destroyers. The convoy coming south from Shortland maneuvered in order to place the task group that was to bombard Henderson Field this night—the *Kirishima, Atago, Takao*, and others—between itself and the American formation. The task group consisted of the three major units with a screen of one light cruiser and six destroyers while one light cruiser and three destroyers were to serve as scouts ahead of the bombardment units. This scouting formation was warned to expect contact with enemy cruisers and destroyers, but critically what it could never have been warned against was a scratch American task group with six units drawn from six different parent formations. This task force was to outfight Kaigun formations in the second of the actions that decided the outcome of the campaign in the lower Solomons.

SUCH A STATE OF AFFAIRS was owed to three realities. The first and most important was the fact that the formation flagship *Washington*, equipped with the most modern radar, had an admiral who understood its capabilities and limitations. Only two nights earlier, ships with this radar had not led and had not been flagships. The second, and scarcely less important, fact was that by mid-November the Americans represented a very different nighttime proposition than had been the case in August. They had purchased experience by their defeats. While over the next year the two sides proved evenly matched in night-fighting technique, by November 1942 the Americans had acquired a certain competence. They may well have been outfought two days earlier but nonetheless had prevented the bombardment of Henderson Field and ensured the destruction of an enemy capital ship, which would suggest a fair degree of familiarity with what was required in night actions. The third and last point related to the advantage of surprise. The Japanese had no inkling whatsoever that the Americans had committed battleships to the defense of Henderson Field. Moreover, each of the two American battleships was superior to the *Kirishima* in terms of gun power and defensive capacity, and the American force was organized simply in line ahead with destroyers leading and knew that any contact had to be with the enemy.

The second naval battle of Guadalcanal, like the first, is sufficiently well known to need no detailed recounting other than the statement of losses, plus three comments on the action. The Americans lost three of their four destroyers and had the *South Dakota* extensively damaged, and the Japanese lost one destroyer in addition to the *Kirishima*, which was ravaged by nine hits with 16-inch shells at a range of about 8,500 yards by the *Washington*. What is surprising about the action is that Japanese lookouts saw the American force more than an hour before the American radar detected the Japanese presence, but their reports were not believed and no credit was afforded later reports that identified battleships in the American order of battle. The *Kirishima* was caught with shells for the bombardment of Henderson Field rather than a naval action, and she, along with her torpedo-carrying associates, might well have won this action. The power failures in the *South Dakota* left her helpless to face the *Kirishima*, and while the American battleship might have expected to survive 14-inch firepower, she most certainly would not have survived massed torpedo attacks.

The *Washington*'s evading detection and then taking an unsuspecting *Kirishima* under attack ensured both the destruction of that battleship and the saving of the *South Dakota*, although in the final analysis the two American battleships were able to make their separate ways from the scene of the action without being subjected to serious torpedo attack. This was the one action in the whole of the campaign in the lower Solomons when Japanese light forces failed both to detect the presence of the enemy—the *Washington*, not the *South Dakota*—and to mount massed torpedo attacks on the enemy main units. Certainly the *South Dakota*, if not the *Washington*, could have been lost to light forces led with only one-half the verve of those that were to maul the American line at the Battle of Tassafaronga a little more than two weeks later. As it was, the belief that more American ships had been sunk than was the case—the force commander claimed to have destroyed one battleship, two cruisers, and two destroyers and probably to have sunk another battleship and two cruisers—may have been a factor in such relatively poor returns on this occasion.

THE CAMPAIGN ON GUADALCANAL had more than seven more weeks to run after the second naval action, but in effect this action— or more accurately this action and the destruction of the transports on 14 November and then the destruction the next day of those that had beached themselves on the island—spelled the end of the Japanese commitment to the lower Solomons. Of course, the campaign continued in the immediate aftermath of the mid-November actions, and the ongoing need to reinforce and supply existing forces on Guadalcanal provided the element of constancy to proceedings following the actions that were fought between 12 and 15 November. The need to maintain their hard-pressed troops on the island forced the Japanese to undertake a resupply run with a scratch force of eight destroyers on the night of 30 November–1 December. Off Cape Tassafaronga this force was caught by an American formation consisting of four heavy cruisers, one light cruiser, and six destroyers, and in the subsequent engagement it lost the *Takanami* but in turn sank one and severely damaged three heavy cruisers. In fact, the Americans won this battle in the sense that the primary mission of the Japanese force, the resupply of troops ashore, was not achieved. But it was a victory indistinguishable from defeat, and the Americans were singularly fortunate not to have lost their entire heavy cruiser complement.

The reality of the situation was not lost upon the Imperial Navy, which on 8 December at a conference in Rabaul informed the local Army command that it intended to halt all destroyer resupply runs with immediate effect. The reason given was the heaviness of losses in mid-November and the fact that if such losses continued, the Navy would not be in a position to fight "the decisive battle" in which it continued to believe until it ceased to exist. In the face of Army protests the Navy was forced to agree to carrying out single supply runs to Guadalcanal and eastern New Guinea, and this was not the end of the argument; the Army made it clear that it would take the matter to Imperial General Headquarters in Tokyo. There the situation was somewhat different in one respect. The Guadalcanal commitment was one that the Imperial Navy had more or less imposed upon the Army, which had always been less than enthusiastic about prospects of victory in the lower Solomons campaign. Moreover, the Army's failures on Guadalcanal could be traced directly to the Navy's inability to properly supply formations ashore which, by mid-December, were losing more than fifty dead per day to tropical diseases and starvation. Thus, the Navy's change of tack—to abandon the struggle for Guadalcanal in order to concentrate upon eastern New Guinea—threatened to precipitate an unseemly row between the two services.

In fact, one other consideration meant that such argument did not pit the Army and Navy against one another. In October 1942 the two were supposed to have returned some 220,000 tons of shipping to civilian service, but the mounting losses in the southwest Pacific theater meant that they requested the transfer of 620,000 tons of shipping from the civilian pool. On 20 November a cabinet meeting sanctioned the transfer of 290,000 tons of shipping to the armed services, and the next day the two were informed by no less a figure than the prime minister, General Tojo Hideki, that meeting their demand would result in steel output in 1943 falling by almost one-half, from an estimated 3,500,000 to 2,000,000 tons. In a series of brutal arguments during December the Army drove Tojo to surrender the shipping it demanded, and in a disastrous case of the undisciplined tail wagging the hapless dog, the Army's immediate operational requirements in December 1942 took precedence over the national ability to wage war in 1943. But as December 1942 progressed, negotiations between Army officers from Tokyo and Rabaul slowly brought home the point that the situation in the lower Solomons had passed recall and that there was no real alternative to abandoning the struggle. The series of small-scale actions fought during the first half of the month cost the Japanese relatively little, but the pattern of sinkings was changing with American aircraft and submarines reaching into the middle and upper Solomons, and in the first twenty-five days of December the Imperial Navy lost seven warships and submarines, and six transports and auxiliaries of various description were lost in theater.

On 25 December the Army high command abandoned the Guadalcanal commitment, and it informed the Navy accordingly the next day. What remained, therefore, was the devising of an alternative strategy for the future and informing the Emperor of the appropriate changes on 28 December. Not altogether surprisingly, there was a distinct lack of agreement between the two services on the critical question of future strategic policy: the Navy wanted to hold the central Solomons, whereas the Army was prepared to abandon these islands in order to stand on a shorter line of communication in the upper Solomons. Such matters were fudged, although the decision to evacuate the men trapped on Guadalcanal was not, and 31 December saw the formal Imperial endorsement of the decision to abandon the campaign in the lower Solomons. In real terms, the campaign in the lower Solomons was over.

III

The

New

Realities

9

THE IMBALANCE OF EXHAUSTION

1 January–15 November 1943

H istories of the Pacific war inevitably gloss over the events be tween the end of the Guadalcanal campaign and the landings in the Gilbert Islands. In this period "nothing happened"— the equivalent of June 1943 in the European theater of operations as the month, with German losses totaling only nineteen tanks and thirty-six assault guns, when the world held its breath at the prospect of what was to come.

It is easy to pass over this period. There were no great shifts in territorial ownership. Certain islands changed hands but none of any consequence, and indeed prior to 1942 few people in Britain, Japan, and the United States would even have heard of most of them. There were no major battles, whether on land, at sea, or in the air. It must be admitted that there were a number of naval actions in the central and upper Solomons, but these were small in scale and none was of any real importance, although one point does demand acknowledgment. The clear American victories at Vella Gulf (6–7 August 1943) and at Cape St. George (26 November 1943) indicate the extent to which Japanese superiority in night fighting, doctrine, and technique had passed.

Acknowledgment of this change is essential to any understanding of the Pacific war because an explanation of this conflict is possible, if only in part, on the basis of this period being a watershed. In the first year or so of the Pacific war two interwar navies fought one another to exhaustion. Initially, Japan's enemies, each individually weaker than its common foe, were defeated separately by a Japan that possessed local superiority and the advantage of the initiative and surprise. In some five months, Japan secured all those territories for which it went to war, and after the defeat off Midway it then settled for a defensive strategy that sought to fight the United States to exhaustion. This strategy was very largely achieved, and a glance at any map showing the changes of ownership of islands in the Pacific or territory in eastern and Southeast Asia between May 1942 and November 1943 will immediately reveal how little progress the Allies made in seeking to reverse the defeats of the first phase of hostilities. But, in fact, after November 1943 the United States, with a fleet that was principally a wartime creation, carried the war to the enemy, and it did so in a way that was remarkable on several counts. Naval wars invariably are slow and seldom noted for speed. The Pacific war lasted forty-four months, which was a remarkably short period for a naval war, and it ended with the Americans having taken war to the shores of the enemy state and, in effect, having defeated that state: American carrier aircraft even flew combat patrols over airfields in the Japanese home islands. Such achievements have few parallels in history, and it is possible to argue that, in terms of decision, the Pacific war ended in November 1943. By this time the United States had come into possession of such margins of superiority in the conduct of amphibious operations that its victory in any single landing operation was assured. The only questions that remained were ones of timing, cost, and the exact nature of its final victory over Japan.

Lest this interpretation of events be doubted, reference to one fact should be noted. In February 1945 five American carrier task groups operated off the Japanese home islands and mustered between them 119 warships: eleven fleet and five light fleet carriers, eight fast battleships, one battle cruiser, five heavy and twelve light cruisers, and seventy-seven destroyers. Of these ships only the fleet carriers *Enter-*

prise and *Saratoga* and the heavy cruisers *San Francisco* and *Indianapolis* fully predated Pearl Harbor, although also present were the battleships *Massachusetts*, *North Carolina*, *South Dakota*, and *Washington* and the light cruisers *San Diego* and *San Juan*, all of which had been launched before 7 December 1941. Any perusal of the lists of warships involved in the landings on Iwo Jima and Okinawa reveals similar pedigree. The battleships detailed to support these landings, but virtually nothing else, predated the Japanese attack on Pearl Harbor; the escort carriers, destroyers, destroyer escorts, transports, and assault shipping virtually without exception were built after 7 December 1941, and it was this achievement on the part of American shipyards that was so relevant in this period between the end of the Guadalcanal campaign and the landings in the Gilbert Islands. This was the time when the first results of this massive building effort really began to deliver warships, assault shipping, and merchantmen in numbers—indeed, in such numbers that Japan could no longer hope to evade final defeat. American merchantman production reached its peak in this period. In March 1943, American yards launched no fewer than 140 Liberty Ships, that is, a 7,176-ton "deplorable-looking object" every 310 minutes. President Franklin D. Roosevelt's description was less than complimentary, but there is no indication that he ever questioned the Liberty Ship's worth. Herein lies the basis of explanation rather than a mere description of events. If one refuses to accept that Japan's defeat was assured from the time that its carrier aircraft struck at the U.S. Pacific Fleet at its base at Pearl Harbor on 7 December 1941, then it was in the first two years of the Pacific war that the basis of America's victory and Japan's defeat was established.

Nonetheless, in setting down such a notion two points need to be noted. First, to recognize that a war is a total one is to recognize that its military dimension can only partially explain its course and outcome. There must also be recognition of the war's nonmilitary dimensions, in such matters as choice of allies and economic issues. But to recognize that a war involves alliances is to recognize that no single nation can ever account for any single dimension of that war. The United States was by far the most important single member of the United Nations involved in war with Japan after December 1941 and it could have completed the defeat of Japan through its own efforts. But that was not the victory that was won between 1941 and 1945. Other powers played their part, at this stage of events none more obviously than China, in contributing to Japan's overcommitment and exhaustion of resources. These aspects of Japan's defeat, over time and distance and of resources, lacked the immediacy and obvious impact of military defeat in the field, and in the final analysis it is the reality of military defeat that decides the outcome of wars. But an intelligent appreciation of both the nature and conduct of the Pacific war lies in recognition of contributions of differing worth and importance.

Second, in seeking to explain events one has to acknowledge the events themselves: explanation does not do away with the need for recounting. In the Solomons the campaign on Guadalcanal witnessed on 10 January 1943 the start of the U.S. offensive that was to result in the clearing of Guadalcanal. American forces landed at Verahue on 1 February, but by this time the Japanese were committed to the evacuation of their forces, which was completed between 1 and 7 February, without the Americans realizing what was at hand. When the Americans did realize what had happened they moved immediately to occupy the Russells (21 February), and at the same time the Japanese defeat in eastern New Guinea assumed an added dimension with the breaking of their offensive from the Mobu area against Wau (21 January–2 February): the Japanese were obliged to withdraw from the Wau area between 3 and 9 February.

Thereafter, events in eastern New Guinea and in the Solomons continued to run in tandem much as they had over the previous five or six months. March 1943 saw a major Japanese defeat in the Bismarck Sea at the hands of American shore-based air power, and also a minor action in Kula Gulf in which an American cruiser-destroyer force sank two Japanese destroyers carrying supplies to the garrison at Vila. Between 7 and 18 April the Imperial Navy, having flown four carrier air groups into Rabaul, conducted what was grandiloquently described as a major air offensive over the Solomons and eastern New Guinea. As always, the Japanese claims of success were grossly exaggerated, and evidence of this fact was provided on 18 April when the Americans shot down a transport carrying Yamamoto to Buin. If the Japanese operation had been successful such an episode could not have happened, but what was even more remarkable about this whole affair is that the Japanese mounted three operations during this offensive—on 7, 11, and 14 April—and with never more than 200 aircraft in any single effort. Moreover, they attacked Lunga Point-Henderson Field and then Oro Bay (near Buna) and Milne Bay in succession. How single efforts against three separated targets, two of which had been stocked by the Allies over seven-month periods, were supposed to reverse recent Japanese defeats is far from clear. But from early June 1943, almost as if they staged a demonstration of how things should be done, the Americans systematically fought for air supremacy over the central Solomons in preparation for a series of landings throughout the theater.

On 21 June, American forces came ashore on southern New Georgia, and then on 23–24 June on Woodlark Island and on 28–29 June on Kriiwana. With the whole of eastern New Guinea thus secured, American forces came ashore on 30 June on Rendova in the central Solomons, near Salamaua and on Woodlark and the Trobriand Islands, off eastern New Guinea, and in Nassau Bay. These actions sparked simultaneous American and Japanese landings in Kula Gulf on 4–5 July and then the naval battles of Kula Gulf (6 July) and Kolombangara (13 July). The American capture of the airfield at Munda, New Georgia, on 5 August prompted the battle of Vella Gulf (6–7 August), and the Americans' crushing victory in that battle paved the way for their landings on Vella Lavella (15 August) and on Arundel Island (27 August).

With the American grip on the central Solomons tightening with every landing, the following month saw the focus switch to eastern New Guinea where the Australians landed at Lae on 3–4 September, while Nadzab saw one of the relatively few airborne landings of the Pacific war on 6 September. The American occupation of Salamaua on 12 September was followed on the 22nd by the Australian landings at Finschhafen, eastern New Guinea. This landing initiated what was for this theater a protracted exchange. A Japanese counterattack was repulsed on 26 September before the Australians moved to occupy Finschhafen on 2 October. This prompted a series of Japanese attacks until 25 October, when the Japanese admitted defeat and evacuated the area. They had read the signs in the Solomons a little earlier and on 20 September completed their evacuation of Vella Lavella and Arundel. Between 23 September and 2 October the Japanese evacuated Kolombangara, where the Americans landed four days later. The latter action provoked the Battle of Vella Lavella, which was really the last drawn battle between the Imperial and U.S. Navies, but no less important was the fact that after 12 October the Americans began their campaign with land-based aircraft aimed at neutralizing and isolating Rabaul.

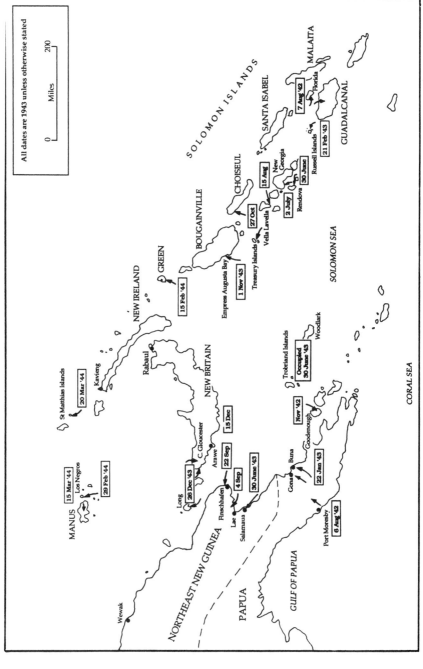

THE SOUTHWEST PACIFIC CAMPAIGN, AUGUST 1942

The whole of the lower Solomons campaign had been conceived and conducted as part of an effort that was to take the Allies to Rabaul, but as the tide of war made its way through the central and into the northern Solomons, this aim changed. The Americans settled on a by-pass strategy whereby the enemy was attacked where he was not, his strengths were avoided, and his forces were left "to wither on the vine." On 27 October there took place the New Zealander landings in the Treasury Islands, and then followed on 1–2 November the American carrier raids over the upper Solomons and the American landings on Bougainville, which induced the Battle of Empress Augusta Bay. In the second half of October the Japanese transferred six carrier air groups to Rabaul to counter the growing American pressure in the upper Solomons, but the raid of 1–2 November, and particularly the raids of 5 and 11 November, had the effect of wrecking Japanese intentions. All the units of a squadron of four heavy cruisers, along with two light cruisers and a destroyer, were badly damaged by carrier aircraft within a matter of minutes of arriving at Rabaul on 5 November, and with the Japanese, in effect, abandoning Rabaul as a naval and air base in mid-November two parts of the American intent came together.

The attacks on Rabaul were part of the effort that heralded not only the end of the Solomons campaign but also the start of the U.S. offensive in the central Pacific. With their victory off Cape St. George on 26 November complementing the landings in the Gilbert Islands, the Americans moved into possession of numbers and technique that ensured victory in every individual enterprise. The Japanese claim that during the November 1943 air battles over Rabaul and the upper Solomons they sank ten aircraft carriers, five battleships, nineteen cruisers, seven destroyers, and nine transports prompts incredulity at the fact that such claims were even entertained, much less given credence. In retrospect they seem almost deliberately to be inversely related to reality.

The start of the central Pacific offensive had been foreshadowed by the American carrier raid on Manus (31 August), on the Gilberts (17–19 September), and on Wake (5–6 October), but if one is obliged to consider the other events relevant to the story then there are four areas of interest that remain to be considered. The first, perhaps naturally, is the north Pacific theater. Here the months that saw growing American success in the southwest Pacific also witnessed American victories that eliminated the Japanese presence in the Aleutians that had been established in June 1942. The only real naval action in this theater, the Battle of the Kommandorskii Islands on 27 March 1943, resulted in the Americans frustrating a Japanese resupply mission to their garrison on Attu. Other than the Battle of the Java Sea, this was the only daylight surface action involving major warship formations of the Pacific war, and it was followed on 11 May by the American landings on Attu. Backed by a massive force that included two battleships, an escort carrier, and seven cruisers, the Americans ensured the collapse of organized resistance on 30 May, the island being declared secure the following day. On 8 June the Japanese high command, recognizing the inevitable, ordered that Kiska be abandoned, and this task was completed on 28 July. In one of the more embarrassing operations of the war American and Canadian forces conducted an assault landing on Kiska on 15 August and fought a series of actions before realizing that the island was deserted. Perhaps the corrective to this singularly sorry state of affairs was the fact that 10 July 1943 witnessed the first American air raid on the Japanese home islands, the Doolittle Raid excepted. The attack, directed against Paramushiru in the Kuriles, was staged by eight B-25 medium bombers operating from Adak via Attu. The last such raid was conducted on 13 August 1945.

The second and third theaters, again where American air power was so important, were Burma and China. December 1942 saw the start of the British offensive in the Arakan, which was brought to a halt short of Akyab in January 1943. On 18 February 1943 the British embarked on the first Chindit operation, a much-proclaimed undertaking that resulted in the temporary interruption of communications between Mandalay and Myitkyina for only as long as it took the Japanese to organize themselves to meet the two attacks. After two months' indecisive fighting in front of Akyab, a Japanese counteroffensive in mid-March resulted in the humiliating rout of the equivalent of a British corps by a Japanese division. At the same time the Chindit units were forced to cross the Irrawaddy and to withdraw to India under intense Japanese pressure. In both efforts the British were decisively outfought, but, as is often the case, in victory were the seeds of Japanese defeat. The fact that the British were able to undertake offensive operations in 1943 after their comprehensive defeat in 1942 prompted the Japanese to consider the possibility of a preventive offensive, a preemptive attack that would forestall a British effort in the 1943–44 campaigning season. Thus, while Chinese forces in northern Burma began an offensive in the Hukwang valley in October 1943 and the following month played host to a second British offensive in the Arakan, the Japanese military settled on "the March on Delhi" that was to end so disastrously at Kohima and Imphal in 1944. This effort compromised the Japanese ability to mount an effective defense of Burma during the November 1944–May 1945 campaigning season.

In the China theater of operations this period saw events that were to be profoundly important in terms of Sino-American relations. The Fourteenth U.S. Air Force was activated on 11 March 1943. The first offensive operation by American aircraft (P-40 fighters) within the China theater was staged on the 16th and the first operation involving bombers was three days later: the targets on both occasions were shipping and installations on the Red River, in French Indo-China. The months of May and June saw a major Japanese raid into western Hupei, and the Japanese withdrawal at its end, deliberately and dishonestly portrayed by the Chinese Nationalists as a major victory, was used by pro-Nationalist and air power lobbies in Washington to support their respective causes. The Tenth U.S. Air Force headquarters at New Delhi, India, began functioning on 20 August while the next day there were the first major air battles in the China theater since 1940–41. These battles were fought over Hangchow, Heng-yang, and Ch'ang-sa, and were followed on 7 October by the first operation by heavy bombers against a target in Burma and on 25 November by the first Fourteenth Air Force raid on Formosa.

By common consent this last operation, against targets in Formosa, represented the point in time when the Japanese high command began to consider seriously a general offensive in central and southern China in 1944. It did so for obvious reasons and with obvious repercussions. The thoughts of the Japanese high command turned to the possibility of a general offensive in central and southern China because it lacked the means to meet and defeat an American bomber offensive: the only counter it could possible employ was the seizing of airstrips from which any such offensive would have to be staged. The implications of this line of reasoning were profound because the Japanese plan, as it took shape, struck at the raw nerve of Sino-American relations.

Much more was at stake at this particular time, in fact, than just relations between Chungking and Washington. These months with which we concern ourselves here, between the end of the Guadalcanal campaign and the landings in the Gilbert Islands (give or take a couple of weeks), saw the Trident Conference in Washington (12–25 May), the Quadrant Conference in Quebec (14–24 August), the first and second Sextant Conferences in Cairo (22–25 November and 4–6 December), and the Eureka Conference in Tehran (28 November–1 December). These months also saw profound changes in the European situation. The defeat of German forces in front of Kursk in July 1943 represented the point where possession of the initiative finally passed irrevocably to the Allies, and the landings at Salerno in September 1943 for the U.S. forces thus engaged represented the first invasion of the European mainland by a non-European army since 1354. Herein were matters of no little import, of considerable meaning and significance. But in terms of China, air power, and the United States, the events in eastern Asia, even if they lacked the grandeur of these other changes, were nonetheless crucially important in terms of relations between China and the United States and the conduct of the war against Japan.

The United States found itself at war in December 1941 wedded to the belief that Japan's defeat had to be total and embrace both the Pacific and the Asian mainland. To this end the Americans were prepared to support China with weaponry, supplies, and money sufficient to ensure the prosecution of the war within that country to the end desired. The Chiang Kai-shek regime at Chungking was eager to play the role of willing recipient of American aid, but it saw as its real priority the civil war against the Communists, which would be resumed once the Japanese were defeated: it had little interest in fulfilling the role that Washington, without consultation, had assigned for it. The American air power lobby, which had come up with the absurd claim that 200 U.S. aircraft based in China could complete Japan's national defeat, had common cause with Chungking: the air force would do the fighting, and the Chinese would hold the airfields. After May 1943 these two interests—the China and the air power lobbies—held the initiative in Washington and prevailed over the various individuals within the State Department and the military who argued that American policy toward China was nonsensical. The military feared a Japanese offensive, believing that Chiang Kai-shek's armies, riddled by corruption and incompetence, would fall to pieces, and there were people in the State Department who feared for American interests by being tied to a regime with so little genuine support among the Chinese people. The conflict between these different factions, and the very real crisis in Sino-American relations that the course of events brought to the forefront of national deliberations, had to await the summer of 1944, but for the discerning and the fearful within the American high command the outline of events was there one year beforehand.

THERE REMAIN ONLY TWO more aspects of the Pacific war to be considered, and these are the nonmilitary dimensions of the conflict that did so much to determine the outcome of the clash of arms. Concerning the first, the war against Japanese shipping, reference has already been made in the Introduction to the fact that in this third phase of the war, between 1 March and 31 October 1943, Japan's defeat was already reality because in this period it suffered shipping losses from which there could be no recovery.

Japanese losses reached a disastrous level above 131,500 tons per month without any contribution to losses being made by carrier-based aircraft: between 1 May 1942 and 31 October 1943, aircraft operating from American carriers accounted for just one transport, while the sinkings by warships were also very modest indeed. The point that is relevant is primarily negative, namely, that if Japanese losses were so disastrous in these periods, then the adjective to describe their losses when the carrier force did contribute was likely to prove very elusive. So it was to be, and for a reason that is often not properly appreciated. The Japanese activated the General Escort Command on 15 November 1943, and it is generally held that the Imperial Navy's creation of this organization, without fully understanding both the principle and detail of convoy and without having sufficient numbers of escorts to properly provide for convoys, meant that it actually worsened the situation: the concentration of Japanese merchantmen in poorly or inadequately protected convoys led to increased losses. That was true, but not until the second half of 1944. The massive increase of Japanese shipping losses between November 1943 and June 1944 was registered primarily not among merchant ships but among naval and military transports in the central Pacific theater, where they were forced to work in waters that were dominated by American carrier aircraft and in which American submarines had concentrated in support of the carrier operations.

The figures tell the story. In the period from 1 March to 31 October 1943 the Japanese lost 109 merchantmen of 376,334 tons, and 160 Army and Navy transports of 676,406 tons: the average monthly loss of shipping of all types other than warships amounted to 33.63 ships of 131,593 tons. In the period from 1 November 1943 to 30 June 1944 the Japanese lost 154.5 merchantmen of 519,187 tons, a significant quickening of the pace. But in this same eight months, 399.5 Army and Navy transports of 1,782,722 tons were lost, and the average monthly loss of shipping of all types other than warships amounted to 89.25 ships of 287,739 tons. Sinkings by submarines increased significantly, from a total of ninety transports of 477,535 tons from 1 March to 31 October 1943 to a total of 225 transports of 1,081,451 tons from 1 November 1943 to 30 June 1944; sinkings by carrier aircraft totaled 76.5 naval and military auxiliaries of 420,337 tons. But even more significant were the returns by area. In the period from 1 May 1942 to 28 February 1943 the transport graveyard was, not surprisingly, the southwest Pacific, but from 1 March to 31 October 1943 transport losses were more evenly distributed, with significant numbers in the East China Sea, the central Pacific, the southwest Pacific, and the southern resources area. In the period from 1 November 1943 to 30 June 1944 total transport losses were 379.5 ships of 1,782,722 tons, with 192 of these transports, of 941,769 tons, sunk in the central Pacific theater. What is no less surprising than the central Pacific toll is the fact that Japanese transport and auxiliary losses in the southwest Pacific were greater in this period than they were between March and October 1943, while losses in the southern resources area also reached disastrous levels, a total of 91.5 naval and military ships of 452,201 tons being lost.

AS IF THE DETAIL OF SHIPPING losses was not bad enough, the second matter to be considered, aspects of national comparison, is one that threatens the poor reader with death by statistics, or at least an ordeal exhausting long before it could be exhaustive. That being so, only two sets of statistics (one naval and the other air) are presented, with minimal comment. First, during the Second World War the United States produced more than one hundred fleet, light fleet, and escort carriers, and the Kaiser yard launched its fiftieth one year and one day after launching its first. In 1943 the United States was building ten destroyers and destroyer escorts to every one launched by Japanese yards, but this modest level of construction on the part of Japan was achieved only at the cost of maintaining the merchant marine. In short, Japan could build merchantmen or warships, or it could build some merchantmen and refit and repair others, or it could build warships. What it could not do was undertake all three on any scale, and the Japanese efforts were utterly inadequate and unavailing. By war's end the American advantage of numbers was overwhelming, and the basis of this numerical superiority was to be found in 1942–43.

In the American and Japanese national aircraft industries the situation with respect to comparative production was the same as that in the shipyards: the United States outbuilt Japan by four to one in aircraft, by nearly seven to one in aircraft engines, and by nearly eight to one in airframe weight. In terms of individual aircraft the basic picture repeated itself. In the course of the Pacific war, Japan produced ninety different types of combat aircraft while the United States produced only eighteen, and, even more significant, in 1943 American factories put out more aircraft than did Japan in the whole of the war. The total number of A6M Zekes (excluding trainers and seaplane derivatives) was (depending on the source) between 10,094 and 11,283, while the United States built 12,272 F6F Hellcats and 12,681 F4U Corsairs. Japanese factories produced 2,446 G4M Bettys while American plants put into the air 9,816 B-25 Mitchells and 12,731 B-17 Flying Fortresses. The latter aircraft was withdrawn from the Pacific theater during 1943 and concentrated its efforts thereafter in Europe, but the B-24 Liberator, with its longer range, continued to serve in the Pacific. With the G5N Sinzan the Japanese had an aircraft that compared very closely to the Liberator in terms of speed, range, defensive firepower, and payload. American factories produced 18,188 B-24 Liberators of all variants. It would be wrong to give Sinzan production in terms of Japanese factories: the entire national output amounted to only six aircraft. Conversely, at peak, in March 1944, American factories were building an aircraft every 294 seconds.

More examples of this disparity could be given, but to no real effect: the situations in the shipyards and aircraft factories serve as indicators of national strengths, and the use of further examples would not add much in terms of explanation of events. Suffice it to note just one matter: that in initiating a war with the United States that Japan knew that it could not win but which it reasoned could be drawn on account of the higher commitment of its people to war, the Japanese high command made one critical error. Clausewitz's words are worth repeating: "the first, the grandest, the most decisive act of judgment which the Statesman and General exercises is rightly to understand [the nature of] the War in which he engages, not to take it for something, or wish to make of it something, which it is not . . . and it is impossible for it to be." And herein lay the Japanese error. If war is a political phenomenon, then it follows that its most important elements are political rather than military or material, but political elements cannot offset material or military deficiencies or imbalances that are too severe. This was the reality that Japan faced in November 1943. For almost two years the United States had found that it had to fight the war in which it found itself as it found it, and not as it would, but by November 1943 the nation, backed by the resources of a continental land mass, was in a position to start to wage the war as it would, and to that Japan had no answer. In part, possession of the initiative had served Japan well in deflecting the United States from its main aspirations, but by November 1941 the advantage that had been Japan's on account of its earlier victories had been spent. From this time, what awaited Japan was the reckoning.

Bibliography

Cook, Haruko Taya, and Theodore F. Cook. *Japan at War: An Oral History.* New York: The New Press, 1992.

Drea, Edward J. *MacArthur's ULTRA: Codebreaking and the War against Japan, 1942–1945.* Lawrence: University of Kansas Press, 1992.

_____. *In the Service of the Emperor: Essay on the Imperial Japanese Army.* Lincoln: University of Nebraska Press, 1998.

Evans, David C., translator and editor. *The Japanese Navy in World War II: In the Words of Former Japanese Naval Officers.* Annapolis, MD: Naval Institute Press, 1969, 1986.

Frank, Richard B. *Guadalcanal.* New York: Random House, 1990.

Hayes, Grace Person. *The History of the Joint Chiefs of Staff in World War II: The War against Japan.* Annapolis, MD: Naval Institute Press, 1982.

Ienaga Saburo. *The Pacific War, 1931–1945: A Critical Perspective on Japan's Role in World War II.* New York: Pantheon Books, 1978.

Miller, John, Jr. *Guadalcanal: The First Offensive.* Washington, DC: Center of Military History, U.S. Army, 1949, 1989.

Milner, Samuel. *The War in the Pacific: Victory in Papua.* Washington, DC: Center of Military History, U.S. Army, 1957, 1989.

Parillo, Mark. *The Japanese Merchant Fleet in World War II.* Annapolis, MD: Naval Institute Press, 1993.

Potter, E. B. *Nimitz.* Annapolis, MD: Naval Institute Press, 1976.

Prados, John. *The Combined Fleet Decoded: The Secret History of American Intelligence and the Japanese Navy in the Second World War.* New York: Random House, 1995.

Stephan, John J. *Hawaii under the Rising Sun: Japan's Plans for Conquest after Pearl Harbor.* Honolulu: University of Hawaii Press, 1984.

Willmott, H. P. *The Barrier and the Javelin: Japanese and Allied Pacific Strategies, February to June 1942.* Annapolis, MD: Naval Institute Press, 1983.

THE U.S. ARMY CAMPAIGNS IN WORLD WAR II SERIES:
Aleutian Islands, 3 June 1942–24 August 1943.
Guadalcanal, 7 August 1942–21 February 1943.
New Guinea, 23 January 1943–31 December 1944.
Papua, 23 July 1942–23 January 1943.
Northern Solomons, 22 February 1943–21 November 1944.

THE U.S. ARMY WORLD WAR II FIFTIETH ANNIVERSARY COMMEMORATIVE EDITION:
  Papuan Campaign, The Buna-Sanananda Operation, 16 November 1942–23 January 1943.

THE U.S. NAVY WORLD WAR II FIFTIETH ANNIVERSARY COMMEMORATIVE EDITIONS:
  The Battles of Savo Islands (9 August 1942) and the Eastern Solomons (23–25 August 1942).

  The Battles of Cape Esperance (11 October 1942) and Santa Cruz Islands (26 October 1942).

Basic Military Map Symbols

Symbols within a rectangle indicate a military unit, within a triangle an observation post, and within a circle a supply point.

Military Units—Identification

Antiaircraft Artillery	⊿
Armored Command	⬭
Army Air Forces	∞
Artillery, except Antiaircraft and Coast Artillery	•
Cavalry, Horse	╱
Cavalry, Mechanized	⊘
Chemical Warfare Service	G
Coast Artillery	⬦
Engineers	E
Infantry	⊠
Medical Corps	⊞
Ordnance Department	⬚
Quartermaster Corps	Q
Signal Corps	S
Tank Destroyer	TD
Transportation Corps	⊛
Veterinary Corps	▽

Airborne units are designated by combining a gull wing symbol with the arm or service symbol:

Airborne Artillery	⌣•
Airborne Infantry	⊠

173

Size Symbols

The following symbols placed either in boundary lines or above the rectangle, triangle, or circle inclosing the identifying arm or service symbol indicate the size of military organization:

Squad . . . .   ●

Section. . . . .   ●●

Platoon . . . .   ●●●

Company, troop, battery, Air Force flight . . . . |

Battalion, cavalry squadron, or Air Force squadron . . . . | |

Regiment or group; combat team (with abbreviation CT following identifying numeral) . . . . | | |

Brigade, Combat Command of Armored Division, or Air Force Wing.   X

Division or Command of an Air Force.   XX

Corps or Air Force   XXX

Army.   XXXX

Group of Armies.   XXXXX

EXAMPLES

The letter or number to the left of the symbol indicates the unit designation; that to the right, the designation of the parent unit to which it belongs. Letters or numbers above or below boundary lines designate the units separated by the lines:

Company A, 137th Infantry . . . .   A ⊠ 137

8th Field Artillery Battalion. . . . .   ⌷ • ⌷ 8

Combat Command A, 1st Armored Division. . . . .   A ⌷⊖⌷ I

Observation Post, 23d Infantry. . . . .   △ 23

Command Post, 5th Infantry Division . . . .   ⊠ 5

Boundary between 137th and 138th Infantry . . . .   —|||— ¹³⁷/₁₃₈

Weapons

Machine gun . . . .   ●→

Gun. . . . .   ●

Gun battery . . . .   ⊔⊔⊔

Howitzer or Mortar . . . .   ⊣●⊢

Tank . . . .   ◇

Self-propelled gun . . . .   ⬒●⊃

Index